*Language
& Philosophy*

Mikel Dufrenne

Language
& Philosophy

translated by Henry B. Veatch
with a foreword by Paul Henle

Indiana University Press
BLOOMINGTON

Acknowledgment

The chapters that follow were presented as public lectures at Indiana University in the fall of 1959 under the auspices of the Mahlon Powell Foundation.

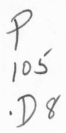

This book has been published with the assistance of a grant from the Ford Foundation.

SECOND PRINTING 1963

To the memory of Paul Henle

Contents

Acknowledgments

I TAKE PLEASURE in expressing my deepest gratitude to my friend, Professor Henry B. Veatch, who translated this book from the French and read the proofs, and to whom I owe so much for many stimulating conversations and for his friendly encouragement. My gratitude also goes to Professor Robert J. Champigny, who assisted Mr. Veatch in the translation.

I wish to thank Professor Newton P. Stallknecht, who kindly invited me to give the Mahlon Powell Lectures.

Paul Henle was for many years my friend; I have no other way of expressing my sorrow than by dedicating to his memory this work, for which he was good enough to write a preface a short time before his death.

M.D.

Foreword

THE RIFT between Anglo-American philosophy with its emphasis on linguistic analysis and Continental thought with its emphasis on phenomenology has become so complete that most members of these groups do not even feel that it is necessary to keep up with what is going on in the other group. The method of formulating problems is quite different on the two sides of the Channel, for few Continental writers would want to pose their problems by asking how certain words are used. The problems themselves seem also to be quite different. Yet there are grounds for believing that philosophy has not simply been split in two or that one group is philosophizing and the other investigating something else under the illusion that it is philosophy. Neither group seems anxious to stress any underlying unity in the problems considered, yet there are striking cases of it. To take only one example, when Sartre says of consciousness at the moment it is present that "it must necessarily be what it is not and not be what it is,"[1] any properly trained analyst shudders, and his horror is hardly abated by the assurance that this paradox applies only to present moments of consciousness and disappears once they are safely past. Such an analyst feels much more comfortable with Gilbert Ryle's claim that there is a systematic incompleteness in terms referring to the self which prevents one from making statements about his own moment of consciousness so long as it is going on.[2] Once it is past, however, there is no trouble in referring to it in another moment of consciousness which, again, cannot find words to refer to itself.

On the surface Sartre and Ryle are discussing quite different problems: Sartre is interested in the nature of the present moment of consciousness, Ryle in the use of certain terms; but underlying both their positions is an agreement that a discussion of one's own present moment of consciousness involves a violation of the rules of logic and of conventional modes of expression. Sartre holds that present moments of consciousness, as present, are so important that they must be discussed, let the consequences for logic be what they may. Ryle, on the other hand, if he ever considered that the ordinary rules might be abrogated, makes no mention of it and prefers to exclude one's own present state of consciousness from the range of discussion. In a sense they are both providing answers, though different ones, to the problem of the possibility and description of the present moment of consciousness. The problem of description, of course, is the problem of correct description, and so the problem of the character of the present consciousness.

The similarity between problems discussed by phenomenologists and analytic philosophers is not always so great or so easy to discover. This gives particular importance to any overt attempt by a member of one group to deal explicitly with problems as formulated by the other. This has happened in the present Mahlon Powell lectures of Professor Mikel Dufrenne. Professor Dufrenne has been trained in the phenomenological tradition and many of his writings are devoted to developing it. With Paul Ricoeur he has written sympathetically on the philosophy of Jaspers.[3] His major dissertation for the doctorate was on the phenomenology of esthetics,[4] and it is along these lines that he has written on the a priori.[5]

In addition, Professor Dufrenne has written on the assumptions of American sociology[6] and has spent a year in this country gathering materials for his study. He has taught at the University of Buffalo and the University of Michigan as well as lecturing at many other schools and, as a result, has had abundant opportunity to discover the temper of American philosophy. He is therefore

able in these lectures to answer from the point of view of a phe-
nomenologist problems in the philosophy of language that have
been of primary interest to analytic philosophers. Thus he discusses problems arising out of linguistics, problems of the relationship between formal logic and language, and even problems
of language and ontology. To say that these questions are an-
swered from a phenomenological standpoint is not to claim that
there is any one answer on which all phenomenologists would
agree, any more than all analysts would agree to the analysis of a
given problem. Professor Dufrenne's conclusions are completely
his own; it is merely that he is working within the phenomenological tradition. Quite remarkably, he has been able to use this
tradition to deal with problems of a very different tradition.

I have stressed Professor Dufrenne's taking cognizance of analytic philosophy because it seems to be of particular importance
at the present stage of philosophy. It would be unjust to his book,
however, to give the impression that this is all he discusses or even
that this is his principal aim. He is interested in many aspects of
the philosophy of language and does not hesitate to take up topics
rarely found in analytic discussions. Thus, for example, he has
provocative comments on the relation of language to thought,
and on the relation of poetry to prose. These and other discussions give his lectures a wider appeal than that of technical
philosophy.

All in all, Professor Dufrenne has contributed to a direct confrontation of two leading schools of philosophy and has done it
in an essay that may be controversial but that will certainly not
be boring. American philosophy will be the richer for this contri-
bution, and the Mahlon Powell Lectureship is to be congratulated
for introducing Professor Dufrenne to the philosophic public of
the United States.

PAUL HENLE

University of Michigan

Introduction

A RECENT BOOK published in the United States and bearing the title *Language, Thought and Culture* opens with the statement: "Language has become an increasingly important field of study during this century."[1] This pronouncement is confirmed, as we shall see, not just by advances in linguistics—advances which, in their turn, have been made possible by advances generally in the sciences of man—but also by the development of symbolic logic and, finally, by the sort of philosophic reflection which, although originating from quite diverse motives, has nevertheless, in the case of Bergson, Heidegger, and the Oxford school, been directed toward language.

Indeed, language has been a philosophical topic ever since the *Cratylus* of Plato. As soon as man turns toward himself, he finds himself speaking. He is a rational animal because he is an *animal loquens,* the only animal who is truly able to speak. I do not wish to raise here the problem of animal language: it is possible that one might be able to clarify certain interpersonal exchanges in the light of animal behavior, much as G. H. Mead attempted to do with respect to the assumption of roles in social psychology. But more often, it is through man that one understands, or believes that one understands, the animal. In any case, animal language is the means of an exchange which is merely vital, and which hence could not be compared with the language of logicians, of poets, or of philosophers. But the very fact that human language could not be derived from animal language, and that its origin remains hidden in the darkness of prehistory, suggests the idea of a transcendent nature of language. And this is the thing that gives rise to philosophical reflection.

Such reflection tends in two main directions: toward an ontology of language and toward a phenomenology of speech. The former conception stresses the powers of language: it is through language that being discloses itself, that meaning emerges; language is then the Word in which Nature—*deus sive natura*—fulfills itself in coming to consciousness. Man, who gives a name to things, is the agent of this fulfillment—the collaborator of God, says Claudel; the shepherd of being, says Heidegger. This idea has been, if not explicitly formulated, at least keenly felt ever since the dawn of civilization. Many primitive cultures express it in myths and magic rites. Nor is there ever a time when man ceases to be amazed at the power that language bestows upon him.

Philosophically, this idea can be translated into a philosophy of nature, as in Schelling, in which the coming into being of the world produces man, who, in turn, carries the world process on to its fulfillment. Again, it can be translated into an ontology, as in Hegel, in which language manifests a Logos that is the dialectical structure of nature, the rationality immanent in nature, and in such a way that the universe of discourse becomes at the same time the discourse of the universe. Finally, this same idea can be translated into an ontology, as in Heidegger, in which language is the abode of being, that in which being both discloses itself and conceals itself. Alike in all these cases, the human being who speaks is not the one who initiates the language; and in speaking, the human being, by his words, accomplishes a purpose that quite surpasses him. Thus it is that the poet and the prophet call themselves inspired; thus it is that Heraclitus can say to his disciples: it is not I whom you listen to, but the Logos.

Nevertheless, it is still necessary that the poet or the philosopher speak, in order that the disclosure be brought about and the destiny accomplished. This is why reflection on language may be turned in a second direction, a direction which I shall follow primarily, that is, that of a phenomenology of human speech, or, if you will, of a study of the human being as one who speaks. Doubtless, we can consider language in itself simply as a given object, be it natural or artificial. And this is the way language is considered both in linguistics and in logic. Still, we shall see that this way of investigating language leads us back to the human being who speaks. It leads us back from the formal to the transcendental. Indeed, it is in this sense that Cassirer—in a way that is almost a parody on Kant—proposes to inaugurate a "Critique" of language. Phenomenology is this critique; it is not just—and Husserl has certainly insisted upon this enough—a psychology pure and simple. We are unable to hold ourselves either to a structural analysis of language or to a psychology of verbal behavior, and this for two very simple reasons.

First, if man speaks, it is because, presumably and at least in his better moments, he has something to say. The question "What do you mean?," so often raised as an objection by the logical positivists, returns like a boomerang against the very empiricism to which this philosophy is so partial: to mean is something more than to react to a stimulus. Nevertheless, the man who speaks never says exactly what he meant to say; and further, he never knows exactly what he meant to say before speaking. To the old formula, "No thought without images," must be added, "No thought without words." The words that I bring forth do the thinking for me, just as the hands of the composer, moving over the keys, do the composing. It is I who think: *ego cogito*. And yet it seems that as soon as I speak, it is language that thinks for me, and the reason is that thought does not have a total mastery of language.

On the other hand, it seems that man does not have a monopoly on speech: if he speaks, it is in most cases because one speaks to him. But who? Others, to be sure, but also the world. Everything can be language, since language is by no means confined to the spoken word. Things can be signs just like words themselves, and they can make signs to us like an interlocutor. This can come about through the play of objective associations, as when smoke bespeaks fire; or it can come about through subjective associations, as where perfume reminds one of a beautiful woman; yet it can also come about through the play of expressions, as when the smile of a mother or of a springtime bespeaks tenderness, or when a certain architecture of a face, or that of the Parthenon, bespeaks nobility. Yes, the power of signifying can belong to the very appearances themselves.

No doubt we are here taking language in a very broad sense, in the sense in which Jaspers is wont to speak of "ciphers." Moreover, taking language in this sense should not cause us to forget that language, as it manifests itself in various tongues, offers us a very definite and precise object: a system of linear sequences, the elements of which are set forth in a lexicon and are organized according to the rules of a particular syntax, a system which permits a certain rationality in meanings and which, in turn, can itself be rationalized through a logical formalism. But perhaps these tongues of which man claims the mastery are themselves founded on a natural language, that is, language in the broad sense of that of which man is not himself the originator. Everyone knows the story of the child who, when someone tells him the names of the stars, inquires in a puzzled way, "But how do we know what their names are? How did they ever tell us?"

This question is not so naïve. Indeed, we shall see how linguistics reflects many variations on the theme of the arbitrary character of language. Thus it could be that the words of a language have an affinity not merely for the total system of the language, but perhaps also for the things themselves which they serve to designate. Poets as well as children invite us to believe as much. Thus the nature of language is as ambiguous as its origin is hidden—at one and the same time, the work of man and the work of the world; both reason and nature. If the Critique of language should be substituted, as Cassirer would like to see, for the Critique of reason, it could only be as a Critique of impure reason. But this impurity is necessary: it signifies that man is bound to the world by an original pact, and that, perhaps, even in cases of the purest reflection, man is never able to renounce this pact.

One can see, therefore, that the phenomenology of speech will lead us back into the domain of a metaphysics of language. Besides, I think that phenomenology can perfectly well be made to accord with ontology, provided that ontology renounces any claims to inspiration from dogmatic theology and that it can be interpreted simply as a philosophy of nature. Moreover, ontology must not aim at depriving man of his power to reveal Nature to itself. Finally, ontology must not scorn the movement by which man tends to emancipate himself in order to fulfill himself and perhaps even to fulfill the wishes of Nature herself.

Our design is, therefore, to reintroduce into the positive study of language the phenomenological perspective, which, in turn, will lead into ontology. And first of all, we shall call linguistics to witness: it treats language as a thing of nature; but this nature is an objectified nature from which man is absent and in which Nature does not express itself. One has to move from syntactics to semantics before one can find genuine human speech once more, as well as that in the world which calls it forth and inspires it.

Next, taking meaning into account, we shall call logic to witness. Here man seeks to make himself totally the master of language, in order that he may make of language the adequate instrument of a *mathesis universalis*. But can language be cut off from the roots that it puts down into nature in much the same way as the formal is rooted in the intuitive? Indeed, from the formal it is necessary to pass to the transcendental and to ask oneself how language is possible. It is then that language becomes the object of a metaphysic of language, the latter being guided by a phenomenology of human speech. And so it is that we shall try to reascend to the very sources of language itself, ultimately tracing speech back to poetry and leaving the final word to poetry.

(1)
Language
& Linguistics

IT IS NOT my purpose to consider in detail the procedures and results of modern linguistics. I should like merely to stress the points that are philosophically significant, because they indicate the limits of the entire enterprise of linguistics and suggest a new and complementary approach. Naturally, I do not intend to criticize linguistics; it does, and does very well, what it is cut out to do. But still, it seems to me, linguistics does not enable us to dispense with a phenomenology of language.

It is well known that modern linguistics renounces the normative point of view of grammar in the older sense, and undertakes a positivistic study of language. Its achievements are considerable. The conceptual apparatus that it has worked out has greatly influenced the behavioral and social scientists, working in their own domains. Some of them, indeed, have even thought that such an apparatus as that used in linguistics could be adopted by other disciplines, in the hope of bringing about a unification of the sciences of man. For the sciences dealing with man are ever on the lookout for a common system of axioms, and their present dispersion and heterogeneity is a veritable scandal from a logical point of view. One need only recall the symposium on anthropology and linguistics held at Bloomington, Indiana, in 1952,[1] when the French sociologist, Claude Lévi-Strauss, who took an active part in the discussion, did not hesitate to propose that linguistics serve as a paradigm for sociology. It is not enough, he maintained, to say that there is a reciprocal relation between language and culture, inasmuch as language is at once a product and a condition of culture. In addition, it must be said that there is a natural affinity between the two, for they are both subject to the same method. We shall return to this theme in a moment.

Phonological Formalization

To begin with, let us recapitulate briefly the principal stages in the development of modern linguistics. The fundamental decision which in a sense inaugurates the whole discipline was taken by Saussure. It consists in distinguishing language from speech, subordinating speech to language and, in consequence, giving a privileged status to syntactics as compared with semantics. One can understand why. Speech is a particular and contingent event, bound to the individual organism. Its meaning, too, depends upon the intention of an individual consciousness. On the other hand, a given language is a positive object, relatively stable and independent of particular circumstances, which I can find in dictionaries and grammars. Likewise, a language is an object which I can observe, as it were, on the surface of the words themselves, when I concern myself not with their content and meaning—with the *lekton* as the Stoics called it—but with their material basis, without paying attention to the peculiarities of pronunciation or of syntactical sequence, but seeking only what is common and, so to speak, necessary in discourse as a whole.

In this way, a language, as distinguished from speech, can be considered as an object that is simply given and that is subject to positivistic methods of investigation. Yet note that what is remarkable about this is that it is possible only if language ceases to be a real object, in the way in which speech is real, and becomes instead an ideal object. By the latter I mean the same as Husserl meant: the ideal object is simply the sense or meaning that one can read from off the surface of the given, provided that one performs the operation of ideation, and this sense or meaning is the truth of the given and always presupposed by the given.

Indeed, from the very fact that speech makes use of a language, speech presupposes a language: there is a certain in-itselfness about language, by virtue of which language is no mere tool for him who uses it, but rather a model. For is not he who speaks forced to obey language and to speak in such a way as to show himself bound by language? Instead of saying that man speaks because he is endowed with organs of phonation, certain biologists prefer to say that man possesses these organs because he needs to speak. This is a little like Bergson, who, in reintroducing a certain teleology into evolution, said that man is endowed by nature with an organ of vision because he needs to see. But it should be added, as well, that man has the need to speak, because language presses toward its own completion. When I speak, the words I use are the realization, more or less imperfect, of the language itself; they are the concretization of an ideal object which is for me at once a starting point and an end to be achieved.

Thus here, again, we find the Husserlian dialectic of origin and of *telos*. Just as, in the order of thought, the essence is at the same time what I am supposed to find at the completion of ideation and what was already immanent in the given, so likewise, in the order of action, language is what I am supposed to produce by my words, but at the same time what was already there before I even started to speak. Similarly, the actor who plays a role is creative without creating, because he realizes a certain model to which he must remain faithful.

But if the ideal object is at the end, how can it be at the beginning? Where, exactly, is this model of the language, or this language as a model, if it somehow exists even before human speech? For the actor, one can say that the model is in the text of the play. But the text has to be interpreted, and what is the criterion of interpretation? The truth of a work of art exists only as a *telos* and an *eidos,* and yet this norm that is so hard to grasp nevertheless functions as an imperative for the interpreter quite as much as for the spectator. The man who speaks is in a similar position: he manifests a pre-existent model. And so, too, the linguist, because, although he defines this model, he does not make it up out of whole cloth like an artificial object or like a system of symbols that the logician constructs. To write a grammar or a treatise on phonetics is in effect to refer to this model. Thus the question remains: where is this model?

One can see that only with difficulty can we avoid getting into an ontology of language. On the other hand, for Saussure, who was trained in the school of Durkheim, the answer is simple: language as an ideal object exists in the collective consciousness, in the *"masse parlante."* This *eidos* is a social essence. It represents a curious convergence of a Platonism on the one hand and a sociologism on the other. But this need not astonish us when we reflect upon it: the Platonic theory of forms is already something whose inspiration is sociological. Be this as it may, however, we still come back to the problem. For the collective consciousness gets its reality from the consciousnesses of individuals, just as culture gets its reality from the individuals who live in that culture and transmit it and modify it. We thus are led back again to the individual speaking and to the phenomenology of human speech.

But first we must examine the principal themes of this positivistic study of language. To consider language as an object is to consider it as a system, that is to say as a reality that is single, autonomous, and coherent, and whose elements constitute a totality governed by laws. Indeed, one easily grasps the idea that each language has its own physiognomy, assembles its own characteristic elements, such as words, and develops its own specific laws. But there is already an ambiguity here: the laws can be either the laws that a certain legislation and tradition have established, or the laws that govern the assimilation of the differentiation of phonemes. Indeed, even the idea of a system in such cases is ambiguous: if a system is a totality, it can be a totality of rules as in grammar (in the classical and narrow sense of the term) or a totality of elements as in the dictionary, or better still, as in the system of phonemes.

In fact, what differentiates these two systems is not that one consists in a grouping of rules and the other of elements, for every system involves both of these. A system is simply an articulated totality of elements subject to certain laws. What distinguishes the two systems is at once a difference in the level of the elements and a difference in the nature of the laws: the grammatical system has to do with words and determines the rules of their arrangement in discourse; the phonological sys tem has to do with phonemes and discloses the laws of their composition in the flow of speech. It therefore seems that the first is truly a system, while the second is rather a field or an area. And yet the system that is constituted by grammar does not truly merit the name: not only are the rules arbitrary, taken just in themselves; but their totality is neither consistent, nor complete, nor saturated. Nor does it take a Gödel to see this. In contrast, however, the field or region that is constituted by the elements of a given language is truly a system, provided one can discern in it a typical structure.

"Structure" is the key word for a type of linguistics that nowadays wants to be a structural linguistics. But this word is, in turn, ambiguous (as is the word "Gestalt," which, depending on the context, can designate the distribution of electrical energy at each point in a condenser, the rhythm of a movement, or the style of a melody). Thus on the one hand, the concept of structure has biological connotations: it can designate an organic unity endowed with a functional individuality, possessing its own proper law of development and its own type of reaction to the environment. On the other hand, the concept of structure can have mathematical connotations: it can designate a mathematical unity, a combinatory system, in which abstract elements are organized according to a certain determinate model. The axiomatization of arithmetic, effected by Peano, defines what is called the structure of a progression. "Structure" thus involves two models that are not isomorphic; and a philosophical problem of great interest is the relationships these models have to each other, and whether the biological model, which is doubtless the more primitive, does not always presuppose the mathematical model.

Linguistics does, perhaps, clarify this problem. If it formalizes language, it is, paradoxically, the better to treat it as a natural object. But nature always preserves certain traits of the Greek *physis*, and that is why we notice that one can speak of a life of language. Nevertheless, linguistics gives a privileged status to that sense of "structure" which, if not exactly mathematical, is at least formal—"structure" conceived as a closed system, in which any change in one element gives rise to changes in the others, and in which the change in the successive states of the system is such as to warrant definite predictions.

But what are the elements that are thus bound together into a totality by the syntactical structure? They are not the specific, concrete words, as traditional grammar suggests. If the structure is formal, the elements that it combines are abstract: they are defined in a manner that is syncategorematic, that is to say not in terms of their own particular properties, but rather in terms of their interrelationship within the system or of their situation within the total field or area; their reality is thus altogether relative and negative. In a language, Saussure says, "There are only differences and no positive terms at all."[2] This is almost what modern epistemology would say about atoms. Thus De Broglie says, in effect, that even in classical physics, "reality seems to be in general intermediate between the concept of an individuality that is entirely autonomous and a system that is completely unified." And, of course, the same would be true a fortiori in a probabilistic physics. This does not mean that abstraction turns its back on the concrete; on the contrary, it is only a detour in order to rejoin the concrete.[3] The ideal object is the truth of the real object, just as the theory of relativity is the truth of the atomic bomb. Still, the concrete that abstraction rejoins and rediscovers is no longer what is given to a naïve perception or to an elementary technique: the atomic bomb is no longer a petard. Thus does linguistics go on to discover another feature of language that is independent of the words: whereas the spoken language is an assemblage of sounds, the analyzed language is a system of phonemes.

Saussure's linguistics in effect ends in phonology. The element is the phoneme, that is to say, an entity which is conceived only in its connection with the total system of the phonemes of the language. Doubtless, it is necessary that there be, if not an individuality, at least a content; but this content is, as Troubetskoi says, "the sum of its pertinent particularities,"[4] that is to say, all the traits which set it over against the other phonemes. Of course, even these traits must be defined in relation to the spoken word, to the sound. They are traits of articulation—thus the "r" can be vibrant, fricative, or rolled. But linguistics stresses the fact that the sound emitted in the chain of words as it is actually spoken is a deceptive point of reference, because it is never anything more than an approximative realization of the phoneme, always charged with a certain slag which comes from the way sound is pronounced and which must be eliminated, in order to bring out properly the pertinent oppositions. That is why certain psychologists, like George A. Miller, prefer to define the phoneme in terms of the actual acoustic datum and by means of spectographic measurements of frequencies.

In any case, as Bloomfield says, "the importance of a phoneme does not stem from the actual configuration of the sound waves, but only from the difference between this configuration and the configuration of the other phonemes in the language."[5] The phoneme is thus essentially defined by the definite relationships that it has with other phonemes: opposition, affinity, possibility of permutation, of substitution, or even of confusion. As a result, the phoneme occupies a certain place in a table of phonemes, in which, just as with the Mendeleev table, certain empty places can signal the probable appearance of a new element. Phonology is thus a combinatory system, "a theory of oppositions," as Troubetskoi says.[6]

Must one then say that structuralism is also a functionalism? The more radical champions of structuralism are suspicious of any functionalism, which strikes them as being a concept at once ambiguous and borrowed from a biological conception of structure.[7] However, it seems difficult to dissociate completely the various ideas of coexistence in a system, of interrelationships, and of function. To reject the idea of function, as Harris does, to exclude all teleology, is at the same time to refuse ultimately to take account of the fact that language does serve a purpose;

likewise, it is to eliminate all reference to semantics. The more moderate structuralists do preserve this reference. For them, the phoneme serves as a means of distinguishing the words, which in turn, convey the sense.

In any case the value of an opposition in any structural scheme is determined by its functional efficiency. For example, in French, the opposition ã õ (*lent* and *long*) is in constant use, while the opposition ɛ̃ œ̃ functions only for two pairs of words (*brin* and *brun, empreint* and *emprunt*). As a result, the latter opposition is probably doomed, for the reason that a scheme that is of little use tends to disappear—in virtue of the famous principle of economy developed by Zipf and first formulated by Passy: "A language tends to rid itself of the superfluous and to stress the necessary."[8] Yet note that semantics in the proper sense has still not been evoked at this level. The phoneme has only to be perceived, that is, recognized as distinct in the midst of an ensemble. It is in this alone that its significance consists: "Its meaning," Troubetskoi says, "is its power to distinguish and differentiate itself."[9]

In consequence of all this, a language can be regarded as susceptible to treatment along the lines of so-called information theory. This, paradoxically, is because a language does not inform us of anything except itself, because through language people can communicate through the transmission of signs, without any meaning being communicated at all. Human communication, in other words, is here reduced to the mechanical communication of quantitatively measured information. Indeed, information theory is an engineering theory. The question is one of how to transmit a message. This message consists of signs that have to be discerned, but that do not have to be understood. For the telegraph operator who sends the cable, it is practically the same thing, whether he transmits the message "Father deceased" or "Father released," but it is very different for the one who receives the message. From the point of view of cybernetics, informing is reduced to the appearance of a selected stimulus in an ensemble of distinguishable stimuli. The content of the information concerns the stimulus that appears and that should be capable of being identified as something distinct; the quantity of the information concerns the field of possible alternatives, the quantity being defined simply as the logarithm of the number of choices.[10] When information is measured by the degree of unpredictability, this in turn leads to a statistical treatment of language. This is seen in the works of Zipf. Moreover, since the distribution of frequencies can be studied in the case of words and syntactical constructions quite as much as in that of phonemes, it becomes possible for lexicography and grammar, along with phonology, to be studied statistically and in accordance with information theory.

The import of these studies, in which structuralism allies itself with cybernetics, cannot escape anyone. Linguistics here accedes to the positivistic age. A language is henceforth an object that is at once theoretically analyzable and practically manipulable. Analyzable, because the structural models can be formalized and treated after the manner of mathematical logic. Manipulable, because the statistical distribution curves of verbal symbols permit the elaboration of semiartificial languages like Basic English, and no doubt, too, the construction of translation machines. But one may wonder whether certain aspects of language are not recalcitrant to this approach, and whether these aspects, at least, do not demand the introduction of quite new concepts. I shall now examine these two points in succession.

Semantics and the Finality of Language

To begin with, still taking language as an object that is independent of speech, it becomes necessary to introduce into it, as it were from the outside, a certain temporal perspective. For structural linguistics neglects, at the outset, the temporal dimension of language. The study of its temporal aspects must needs come after the study of it as nontemporal, and one can understand why. As soon as language is considered as a system, an ideal object, it is a timeless object: its essence is not subject to the vicissitudes of existence. Take the game of chess: to know the game, one has to learn the rules; and the rules, just like any rules of syntax, are nontemporal or, in any case, as Husserl says, omnitemporal. They are valid for all times and for all places. In contrast, when two players actually engage in playing chess, this is an event in history: each move that is made follows the one before within a concrete duration. Nevertheless, even now, each moment of the game constitutes a momentary system. To understand it, it is necessary to consider the game as a whole whose elements all fit together and where any movement of the one element affects all the others. Doubtless, each move forms part of a history: it is conditioned by what has gone before in the game and it is oriented toward what will come afterward; it opens certain possibilities and it closes others. But the sort of time that pertains to the course of the game is still not something of concrete duration: it is, like Cartesian time, a succession of discontinuous instants; the link that unites the moves of the game is logical rather than chronological. One does not explain a game by saying how long it has lasted or by recounting a history, but rather by making a logical analysis. It is just this that linguistics has undertaken primarily to do. An individual word, for example, is not something to be explained by its history or its etymology, but by its place and function within the system. Indeed, the only interesting etymology is the false etymology, the sort of popular etymology of which ‚Plato gives examples in the *Cratylus:* and this is because such an etymology is founded on an obscure consciousness of associations and syntagmas that are suggested by a given state of the language. Thus linguistics abstracts from all becoming. Indeed, one might say that from the point of view of such a one as Saussure, linguistics is Cartesian before it becomes Leibnizian.

And yet there is, quite incontestably, a life of language, and it is this life which imposes upon one the idea of a certain teleology. Thus Martinet, who returns explicitly to a temporal perspective in his book on *L'Économie des changements phonétiques,* speaks of an "optimum state" of the phonological system, in which each phoneme would be at once clear and distinct, necessary and sufficient. And already Troubetskoi has spoken of a "tendency toward harmony." No doubt, the linguists are able to conceive of this harmony in a way that is

purely mechanical: it is the state of stability of the system—
for example, of the system of phonemes—at a given moment.
This stability is all the greater as the system is clearer and
more economical. It is the result of a compromise between two
opposed exigencies: on the one hand, the need for information,
which requires that the signs be less redundant and consequently
that one utilize as widely as possible the pertinent articulatory
types; and on the other hand, the principle of inertia, which requires, on the contrary, that the unities be more general and less
numerous, and which is due to a certain spontaneous laziness
on the part of the speaking human being, as well as to the
biological fact of the asymmetry of the vocal organs, as a result of which certain phonetic combinations are simply ruled
out. As Zipf says: "Linguistic evolution in general may be conceived as governed by the permanent antinomy between man's
need for communication and expression and his tendency to
reduce to a minimum his mental and physical activity."[11] However, the compromise is never definitive; the equilibrium is
never stable.

The factors of instability are twofold. They may be internal:
for example, the degree of integration of the phonemes, the
attraction exercised by the system on each element, the risks of
confusion between the various distinctive unities. Or they may
be external: the ceaseless action exerted upon the system by the
linguistic environment, analogous to the phenomena of "culture,
contact, and change" as studied by Malinowski.

But this explanation of the evolution of language, although it
is still structuralist in character, evokes a certain finality, if the
incessant structuring of a language tends toward a form that is
held to be perfect and yet that is ever being called into question.
And the problem then becomes: just where does the goal or end
of language reside? From the point of view of structural linguistics, a language is an autonomous object, obeying its own
laws and pursuing its own end quite independently of the human beings who use it, who are, in a manner of speaking, only
the means or the instrument for the language's own proper realization. Paradoxically, linguistics would thereby seem to re-
habilitate that very biological conception of structure which it

formerly denounced, on the ground that in such a conception a language was considered as if it were a nature endowed with its own internal power of evolution. Nevertheless, linguistics must needs take account also of the human beings who speak the language, for it can scarcely avoid invoking the attitudes that they have in regard to the language and the services that the language expects from them. Linguistics should, therefore, admit that a language has its end outside itself in speech. To be sure, the immediate causes of change are internal to the system, as in the processes of self-regulation; but the principle of finality is external to it. Thus Jakobson says that "in fact, language is an instrument made for and subordinate to the concepts which it is supposed to express."[12] It is therefore in principle subordinate to thought. Its value cannot be defined solely in formal terms by the cohesion of the system of unities at once distinctive and integrated; instead, it is measured by the services that it renders to thought.

If this be the case, then—and this is my second point—the most important branch of linguistics should be semantics. Semantics, though, is generally neglected by the structural linguists. For example, attempts, like that of Trier, to work out a structural semantics bear only on very limited sectors of vocabulary and are not decisive. And one can understand why. The theory of information, to which the structuralists subscribe, considers language as an object of communication rather than as a means of communication. Moreover, structuralism itself deals with signs rather than meanings. The meaning is reduced merely to the distinct apprehension of sounds, as if the only problem were to transmit or register a message properly without having to interpret it or decode it.

And yet, to have an ear that is sensitive and experienced enough to recognize Chinese phonemes and to receive a message in Chinese correctly is still not to understand Chinese. Certainly, as Lévi-Strauss suggests, linguistics should rid itself of a certain lien with which it has sometimes been encumbered; it should renounce the idea that there is any internal necessity that unites sound and sense. But it hardly suffices for this merely to recognize "that the significatory function of a language is not directly tied up with the sounds themselves but with the way in which the sounds are combined with one another."[13] For the sounds combine to produce words or phrases to which a meaning is attached, and in order to know the meaning, one must know more than just the elements of the language and the system of their combination. What is signified is of a different order from that which does the signifying, in the sense of fixing the meaning and communicating it. Just as Spinoza said that the idea of the circle is not itself round, so one may say that the word "circle" is still not the idea of the circle.

Later on we shall return to the psychological problem of the relations between language and thought. For the present, however, let us merely note that the preceding remarks exclude any sort of behavioristic solution, at least to the degree that such a solution tends to consider the verbal sign as an arbitrary signal whose meaning excites a response but does not elicit anything like understanding. To be sure, information theory often goes hand in hand with a behavioristic psychology. And this is perfectly legitimate when one is analyzing a segment of behavior, such as that of a workman at his work, which is regulated by certain directions regarding the job to be done.[14] Of course, if the foreman chances to make some remark to the worker, he will react to that, too, much as he reacts to the condition of the object on which he works. But his reaction is not called forth in the same way, for in this case it proceeds by way of an understanding of the meaning attached to the words that the foreman utters.

Let us continue to consider language as independent of the spoken word. How can signs convey and transmit a meaning? To this question linguistics alone cannot provide an answer. If an answer is possible, it can be only by means of metaphysics. Still, linguistics can clarify the question. First of all, from the point of view of semantics, the units that do the signifying are no longer phonemes but words. Doubtless the spoken chain, as it is emitted or recorded, does not permit any rigorous discernment of the words; in French, "sižlaprã" may be analyzed in two ways: "Si je l'apprends" and "Si je la prends." From this sort of thing arise all those ambiguities and equivocations that must be the bane of inventors of translation machines. But if such ambiguities amuse us, it is precisely because we are attentive to the words, and because we come across words with an unexpected meaning in place of words with the expected one. Semantically, the unit is thus indeed the word. Nor does the fact that words are tied into phrases which we apprehend as totalities, nor even the fact that the meaning of the words is determined by and tends to change with the context, prevent the word from having a personality of its own and from being fundamentally the repository of the meaning.

Still, the word has this function only as an element of the whole. And the whole is not so much the phrase or the sentence as the entire language. Indeed, the question once more suggests itself, as it suggested itself to the Greeks: if the word has a meaning, does it have such a meaning *physei* or *thesei*, by nature or by convention? Short of an answer in terms of metaphysics, which in turn would presuppose an entire philosophy of nature, the first answer linguistics would be tempted to give is that—following the dictum of Saussure—verbal signs are arbitrary. Otherwise, how would such a thing as the confusion of Babel be possible? And how in a given language would the existence of such things as homonyms and synonyms be possible?

Such an overly simple notion, however, needed to be corrected, and it was corrected by Saussure himself. The arbitrary character of language is partly neutralized by what he terms "motivation." Such motivation can be purely phonetic, as is the case with onomatopes and merely expressive words. And yet the motivation itself may well be arbitrary in turn: if the *tic-tac* (in English, "tick-tock") of a clock may be considered as motivated, what is one to say of the "tactics" of a general? If, in French, *ombre* is motivated by the desire to express the depth and weight of darkness, what is one to say about *concombre?* Similarly, Mallarmé remarked that it is the word *jour* which is somber, while the word *nuit* is bright and joyous. To be sure, to try to make very much of such correspondences as poets find is likely to seem altogether arbitrary, simply because the poet's interpretations are so often purely personal. (And yet there is a core of truth here, which we shall come back to later on.)

But such motivation may be morphological as well as phonetic in character. "Thirteen" (sc. three ten) is more motivated than "eleven." "Armchair" in English is more motivated than *fauteuil* in French. And in general, French is a language that is not very motivated in this sense. That is why it does not lend itself very readily to anything like the development of a "Basic French": it is full of all sorts of technical words that give to its vocabulary an abstract character.

Over and above such motivations, there is a kind of general motivation that is difficult to define simply because one can experience it only through placing a word within the totality of the entire vocabulary of the language. Thus when one learns a foreign language—and perhaps it may even be the case with one's mother tongue—there comes a time when, after all the analytical studies of vocabulary and grammar, one becomes familiar with the over-all aspect of the language. One has, in short, acquired a feeling for its semantic structure, a structure that cannot be formalized in the manner of phonological structures and that is capable of being recognized more by feeling than by understanding. Indeed, it is much like the way in which one perceives the structure of a living organism—the bodily structure of a snake or a crustacean, for example. As a result, one finds himself moving about in the language as in familiar surroundings, no longer mistaken about the meanings of words. One comes to appreciate the nuances enough to choose the right word from among the synonyms. And the sense or meaning of the word seems to belong to that word naturally and in consequence of its insertion in the linguistic totality. The word has, in fact, an expressive aspect that no longer depends on a phonetic motivation, because it stands out as a necessary force against the background of the language. If we consider the word to be expressive by nature, it is in no wise the nature of things, the *natura rerum,* but rather the nature of the language that we must invoke. The reason is, moreover, that this nature of things is known to us only through the medium of language. In other words, language is indeed motivated, but only because it is self-motivated and because it employs a kind of internal logic.

In effect, just as the word is significant, so this background of language as a whole is significant. To be master of a language is to move within a certain universe of meaning; and it is here that semantics rejoins cultural anthropology. Cultural anthropology has long noted that each language offers a veritable *Weltanschauung,* an implicit vision of the world. One is familiar with the way in which Cassirer developed this theme in a Bergsonian setting: the given is a confused and moving chaos that the words and the syntax serve to organize; we view the spectacle of the world more with our words than with our eyes; we think of the world far more as a function of our syntax and verbal habits than as a function of any objective relations that we might immediately find in it. No, in this view, it is necessary to renounce the idea of pure fact. No one is ever content with the business of merely "pointing at." Instead, one always speaks, and at once a whole way of thinking, incarnate in the very language, precedes and goes beyond the individual thought. Thus our physics is oriented by our logic, and our logic by our grammar.

Language and Culture

Having reached this point, we immediately find ourselves confronted with a new problem: this is the problem posed by the extraordinary diversity of languages. Even if we take into account the lexical and grammatical similarities that exist between languages proceeding from a common hypothetical ancestor, the fact remains that the verbal universe is divided into multiple sectors. Sapir, Whorf, and many others, comparing the Indian languages with the Occidental languages, have underlined this diversity very forcefully. It seems, indeed, as if the arbitrary character of language, having been shown to be of comparatively little significance at the level of the elements of a language, reasserts itself quite definitely at the level of the language taken as a whole. And if one admits that a language represents a kind of destiny, so far as human thought is concerned, this diversity of languages leads to a radical relativism.

As Peirce said, if Aristotle had been Mexican, his logic would have been different; and perhaps, by the same token, the whole of our philosophy and our science would have been different.

The fact is that this diversity affects not only the languages, but also the cultures, that is to say the whole system of institutions that are tied to the language—religion, science, technology, ideology, and even family relationships and social stratification. The problem is thus posed for anthropology to determine in the case of each society the relationship between the language and the totality of that society's institutions. Nor can this relation be conceived as a causal one, as Cassirer suggested. For this would imply a philosophical theory that would be quite as debatable as, from another point of view, would be a materialism that failed to be a dialectical materialism after the manner of Marxism. To anyone who would attribute to language so considerable a causal power, one can always answer that language in its turn is the effect and the expression of a certain world view that is manifested in the culture. If there is causality, it is a reciprocal causality, and any positivistically-oriented study should limit itself to the mere description of a parallelism. But this correspondence itself scarcely gets beyond the commonplace. For just how is one to grasp it and systematize it? Perhaps one should once more have recourse to the perspective of the structuralist.

Here it would be well to follow the lead of Lévi-Strauss. He reproaches Whorf for having sought correlations between two terms that have been unequally analyzed. For while the language may be studied with precision by linguistics, the culture is subject to only the crudest sort of observational techniques, particularly when it is considered in its totality.[15] If structuralism simply fails in this connection, it is because the structures of the cultural system are not really known. Besides, Lévi-Strauss proposes a more modest task: a confrontation of the linguistic structures, not with the structure of the culture, which, after all, simply cannot be determined, but rather with certain structures that are proper to certain particular institutions. Such can be considered as partial expressions of the total culture: for example, the rules governing consanguinity or the various mythical representations. Such structures are, of course, but partial models, being "local" in character and in a sense frequently "conjectural."[16] But does not structure exist whenever terms are put in relation to each other within the confines of a closed system? May not one say that a large part of the activity of human beings is to be traced back precisely to a threefold exchange, of words, of women, and of goods? (To which one would need to add "symbols" and "concepts," if the semantic structures are not to be reduced to morphological structures. This is just what the analysis of myths might be said to attest to.) And may not one then search for certain homologies between the formal properties of these different systems of exchange?

The types of structure characteristic of a given culture would then, in each case, be particular modes of universal laws. They would define the *Volksgeist* and would even authorize a logico-mathematical treatment of nothing less than the Hegelian idea of objective spirit, considered as a specification of the absolute spirit and as at work in history. A grandiose idea, certainly. However, the research would not seem as yet to have led to any very decisive results. Still, the way has scarcely been opened, and one ought not to prejudice in advance any results to which it might lead. In any case, it is necessary to give credit to Lévi-Strauss for having opened up this way.

All the same, one cannot but be sensitive—for the time being, at least—to two difficulties. First of all, there is the difficulty that is suggested by the one essay that Lévi-Strauss has attempted with a view to bringing about a confrontation of the structures of consanguinity with the structures of language.[17] That difficulty is that the homologies between the structures of systems so very different from each other can manifest themselves only at the price of extreme abstraction. It is as if one had to liquidate the whole of the concrete content of these structures in order to make them susceptible of formalization. And then the structures would seem to have lost the better part of their sense and meaning. Indeed, one may well ask whether they can be formalized at all with impunity. Does their logical sense not wholly eliminate their biological sense? If, furthermore, they inevitably take on a particular meaning and significance

depending upon the particular domain to which they are applied, then are they not, after all, simply incomparable?

Structural analysis is here in danger of succumbing to the
temptation of ontologizing the purely formal. And then the
theory is caught in its own trap. To be sure, every science attains the real only in and through a conceptual apparatus,
and structural analysis is possibly the most rigorous and the
most fruitful of such types of apparatus. But one must take care
not to project the formal structures onto reality, nor to forget the
specificity and the diversity of the material structures. Indeed, this may well be what happens when one tries to assimilate
to an unconscious spirit or Geist the various cultural structures
between which, through formalization, certain homologies have
been revealed. Certainly, each culture has its own genius,
and it is an admirable undertaking to seek to deal with it posi-
tively and scientifically. But as soon as one defines this as an
unconscious logos that brings into being a specific, logical form
of the culture as a whole, is not one thereby simply creating an
object that is no more than the projection of the anthro-
pologist's own logical operations? It is then that one pretends to
discover in the object what in fact one has only put there oneself.

It is only fitting, therefore, that one should be attentive to the
diversity of the material structures, as well as to the resistance
that the real always seems to offer to structuration. The real, of
course, is more or less susceptible to being structured, and the
structure is more or less real. Indeed, to come back to the matter of language again, it does seem as if the structures of the
phonological domain were different from the structures of the
semantic domain. The former make it possible to explain a system of distinctive unities; the latter make it possible to understand a discourse. In the former case, the structures bind together signs that do not yet have, or no longer have, any intentionality of their own, and whose combination amounts
either to a purely formal logic or simply to a game, like the
game of chess.

The structures of the semantic domain, however, bind together
signs that signify either equivocally, like the words in a myth, or

univocally, like the concepts of physics. And what the combination of these signs intends is to bespeak a reality either sacred or profane. However, since such a combination of signs takes place without any combinatory system, can one say that it is even a structure? Does the meaning that is presented by the ordering of reasons or by the movement of the drama reside any longer in the structure? Likewise, is to comprehend the meaning simply to disclose a structure? Here one would really need to call Lévi-Strauss to witness against Lévi-Strauss. In the admirable analyses of myths which he has published,[18] there is most certainly a structure that ties the symbols together. Indeed, this is analogous to the oppositions of characters in a drama or the oppositions of events in a sequence. And yet the sense and meaning are derived primarily from the significance of the symbols that Lévi-Strauss interprets with all the resources of a comprehensive psychology and sociology. In short, it can be said that while the structure brings the symbol into play, it does not confer upon it a sense or a meaning.

There is no doubt, of course, that phonological reality admits of structuration more readily than semantic reality. And before one goes to the length of invoking an unconscious logos, at work alike in the spoken word and in the institution, one should perhaps first clarify the lived meanings that are experienced by the men speaking the language. In any case, one should join to any logic of the language a phenomenology of the spoken word. Moreover, this phenomenology will, in its turn, rediscover the idea of a logos immanent in the language; but it will seek the justification for this in a more general philosophy of the relations between man and the world. It is there, in such relations, that language finds its origin, and it is there, in the same context, that language may be said to be natural.

This, moreover, is the reason why we do not think that the diversity of languages or even the diversity of cultures is the last word. Today, cultural anthropology (note the example of Kluckhohn) insists upon a human basis and background common to every culture. Man always recognizes man, if not as his neighbor, at least as his like. Indeed, the stranger is strange, and sometimes even redoubtable, only because he is an alter ego.

From one culture to another it is possible to establish communications. The Rorschach test has been successfully applied to the natives of the island of Alor. And tribes still in the Stone Age are able to master very quickly the most modern techniques. So far as language is concerned, at least approximate translations are always possible: the diversity is not irreducible. What separates is always in the first instance the same as what unites: everywhere man is a creature who speaks; hence whatever the diversity of languages may be, they at least have in common that they are spoken; and this, in turn, implies that everywhere man has the same basic relation to the world. Indeed, it is the exigencies of this very relation that are responsible for man's being man everywhere and for such a thing as humanity to be possible. Similarly, one must needs come back again from the study of language to the study of speech, because language is nothing more than a mediation between man and the world. One can, certainly, and one ought to treat it as an object that is susceptible of a structural analysis. But still, this object does not have its end in itself: it is ordered in its power of signifying; nor is the signification of which it is capable conferred upon it by the structures that organize it and render it distinct. Signification brings into play the relation of man and world, and in the final analysis, it is this relation that philosophy should reflect upon in order to do justice to language.

Such will be the subject of our third chapter. But first of all, it will be necessary for us to put to the test the idea that language is natural. And the way we propose to do this is to confront the common language with the artificial language elaborated by logic.

(2)
Language
& Logic

IN THE PRECEDING chapter we insisted upon attributing to semantics an importance that structural linguistics is tempted to neglect. Man speaks in order to say something, and in view of this fact he is quite naturally inclined to regard language as an instrument in the service of thought, and to regard thought as something whose value is measured by its truthfulness. One can, no doubt, sustain the inverse view, according to which man is regarded as saying something only because he speaks. And then, as a consequence, it will be the truth of language that will be regarded as measuring the value of thought. This latter idea is acceptable, perhaps, so long as one does not join it to another, to wit, that the truthfulness of language rests only on usage, and that as a result the thought, which is incarnated in language, is relieved altogether from having to bring itself into accord with reality. It is just such a juncture of ideas that the Oxford school has effected in following the maxim of Wittgenstein:[1] "Don't ask for the meaning, ask for the use." This, indeed, is why Gellner's[2] reaction against "the later Wittgenstein," like Russell's, would seem to be a healthy one.

No doubt the Oxford school might well be justified if, in the first place, instead of seeking a unilateral relation of language to thought, it set up a reciprocal relation between them, and if, in

the second place, in order to clarify the truthfulness and re-
liability of language, it sought to base language on man's relation
to the world. This is the road, indeed, that I propose to follow
myself. But meanwhile, it will be necessary to consider thought
in its role as judge of language and to assess the power that
thought claims over language insofar as thought undertakes to
create a logic. For such a logic is not the logic that is implicit in
ordinary language, nor a logic of usage,[3] as it might be called, but
rather it is the elaboration of a new language, requiring an altogether new usage.

The Démarche of Logic

The truth is that among philosophers language arouses
as much suspicion as confidence: not only is the diversity of languages disconcerting, but one's mother tongue itself is accused
of being a deceiver. Descartes already stated in the "Second
Meditation": "Words nevertheless impede me, and I am almost
deceived by the terms of ordinary language. For we say that we
see the same wax if one presents it to us, and not that we judge
it to be the same on the ground that it has the same color and
the same shape."[4] But, prudent as Descartes was, he has been
reproached for having betrayed his own *cogito* when he spoke
of *res cogitans,* thereby confounding the transcendental ego
with the psychological ego.

What is more, logical positivism, for its part, quite as much as
Bergson—albeit in a totally different perspective—denounces
the illusions that are created by language and the perpetual
temptation to take properties of words as being properties of
things. Indeed, the most celebrated example of what Russell
calls the "fallacy of verbalism"[5] is the introduction of a substantialist ontology, suggested by the grammatical relation of subject
and attribute, which is common to the European languages.*

* Such an interpretation of the grammatical origin of substantialist ontology is nevertheless debatable, as we shall ourselves see in the ensuing
chapter.

Even so, the structure of their own language has apparently not prevented certain European philosophers from setting up a philosophy of becoming in opposition to a philosophy of substance. Thought, in other words, is not wholly necessitated and bound by language. And yet the fact remains—and we have already observed as much—that every language implies a vision of the world that burdens philosophic reflection. Indeed, the adversaries of philosophy can always counter with Hamlet's retort, "Words, words."

Accordingly, it is not hard to understand how man tends to be astonished and abashed in the presence of language and how, after an initial moment of reverence, he has been seized by a nostalgia for a universal language, which would deliver him at once from the confusion of Babel and from the profusion of purely verbal fallacies. Not infrequently it must have seemed as if a veritable Paradise Lost had been evoked by the linguists as they delve into the past in their search for roots and origins. But equally, it must seem to be a Paradise Regained that is promised by the logicians when they pretend to throw open the future with the construction of a new language. Indeed, ever since the Renaissance the development of science and particularly of mathematics has revealed the power of reason over language: new names have been invented for new objects; new morphemes for new relations; a new syntax for a new rationality. And all the while, the moat that separates science from perception becomes ever wider and deeper. For science is more than just ordinary language plus various technical terms. Instead, it involves a new language, which, in turn, brings into play a new logic. Moreover, it is just this fact that gives the impetus to those grandiose Leibnizian projects for a *characteristica universalis* which might serve as the instrument of a truly rational calculus, that is, of an infallible language that would actually do one's thinking for one. As Leibniz himself remarked, once we are possessed of this new language, we won't have to do a lot of discussing and arguing behind the scenes when confronted with a problem; we will need only to sit down and calculate. This sort of Leibnizian project has been taken up once again by the modern logicians, who arrogate to themselves an absolute power over language by simply creating an artificial language. As Carnap says: "A logical system is not a theory, that is, a system of assertions bearing on determined objects; rather it is a language, that is, a system of signs with the rules for their use."[6]

It seems that we are here truly very far from the traditional conception of logic. For Aristotle, logic is an *ars demonstrandi* rather than an *ars inveniendi*. It aids us in putting ordinary language to a more rigorous use by correcting it and by better utilizing its resources. But it does not invent another and different language. What is more, the rules that Aristotelian logic lays down are not products of an arbitrary choice, but reflect the nature of being. And the reason they do so is that such a logic presupposes a tacit agreement between language and being: language is true and is a condition of truth, because it is the language of being and its norms proceed from being.

If, on the other hand, in contemporary logic the rules of language are held to proceed not from being but from man, then what assurance is there that such language will be true? If "in logic there are no morals,"[7] how can there be any truthfulness in a logic so conceived? On such a question, let us at once declare ourselves: this nominalism cannot be the last word; we simply cannot renounce the hope that our logic should be true. Indeed, even Wittgenstein would seem not to be so far from Aristotle when he writes in the *Tractatus* (2.18) that if a sentence is to assert a fact, there must be something in common between the structure of the sentence and the structure of the fact. This is why the study of morphology and syntax can inform us as to the structure of the world. (One knows how much this theme has occupied the attention of Oxford philosophers. And yet their concern would seem to have been not so much to sharpen this theme as to blunt it. For in their eyes, the study of linguistic usage tends to replace and even to enable one to dispense altogether with the study of the truth claims of language.)

Nevertheless, existing languages are diverse and are always, as Russell says, insufficiently logical. As we have already remarked, they tend to inflect human thought in the direction of a certain vision of the world, the objectivity of which, in view of its relativity, is always contestable. It would seem, therefore, that it is necessary to create an ideal language—that is to say, a language which can mirror the structure of reality. One has, after all, ever since Aristotle, supposed that the structure of reality is logical. Still, the problem is: how can we assure ourselves that the language that we create will be a good language in this sense? This difficulty has been clearly seen by Copi: "The project must have the following sequence: first, an 'ideal' language must be set up and *then,* through it, the metaphysical structure of the world is to be discovered. . . . But this program cannot possibly be realized, because the only way to tell of a given language that it is 'ideal' is by comparing its structure with that of reality. For this comparison to be significant, we must have prior and independent knowledge of the structure of reality. . . . The proposed program involves a vicious circle and must therefore be rejected."[8]

In the face of this difficulty human thought is tempted to return either to the nominalism of Carnap or to the empiricism of Oxford. However, I do not believe that this vicious circle is inevitable. The difficulty appears only if one does not correct Aristotle by means of Kant, and if the program does not moderate its ambition to grasp reality as it is in itself. For reality is always reality for us, grasped in and through verbal forms. Hence a dialectical relationship is possible between the amelioration of language and the amelioration of knowledge. Language discloses reality to the extent that reality confirms language. But this presupposes a first language, or a natural language, and an accord between this language and the world, which is in itself the miracle of speech. Accordingly I shall attempt to show that even a logical language corresponds to reality, that is to say to the formal aspects of the real. And yet because such a language never manages to achieve a complete abstraction, it is always founded on natural language. Indeed, whenever man undertakes to form an artificial, logical language, he inevitably finds that at the same time he is himself being formed by the natural language.

For the moment, however, we must proceed in the opposite direction, following the efforts of logic to construct a new language and attempting to render justice to the extraordinary prowess of logical formalism. In truth, traditional logic itself moved in this direction, at least to the extent that it constituted a formalism. And, after all, logic does interest itself only in form, inasmuch as—and Aristotle was the first to realize this—the validity of an argument is a formal property, based on form alone and discernible from the formulation itself. Such formulation must needs be governed by laws, which define and guarantee the validity of the inference. In consequence, logic is a syntax before it is anything else, a system of rules for the manipulation of the terms. Nevertheless, modern logic goes a step further in affirming, at least most of the time, that these rules are arbitrary. Moreover, in the light of this development, it becomes clear that the validity of the formalism must be distinguished radically from its truth. In order that an inference be valid, we have to be consistent only with ourselves and not with the real. Our language thus becomes correct, but empty. And logic as a whole becomes merely a game, like a game of chess: we conform to the rules, but the rules do not have to conform to reality.

But let us not go too fast. Modern logic is a symbolic logic. It introduces symbols that are the elements of a new language, just as arithmetic introduced the Arabic notation, and albegra letters in place of numbers. But a symbol is not simply an artifice of writing; it is a sign charged with significance. What then does it signify? It would seem that in symbolic logic, a symbol will signify either terms on the order of predicates or propositional functions, or relations between such terms, when the signs are operators that permit a logical manipulation. In both cases the symbol signifies indifferently and in the manner of a variable, or like a Leibnizian character—that is to say, simply as an element in the calculus.* In contrast, a signal such as a

---

* One can further observe here how the logical symbol is taken in a sense that is rigorously opposed to that of the symbol which animates mythological or metaphorical language. When one says, for example, that "Night" or "Tree" or "Sky" are symbols, one means that these words have a sense that is doubly concrete. They are tied to a primary content, and then, through this and, as it were, transparently, they are tied to a second content. Nor is there any way in which this double content and meaning can be translated. As Paul Ricoeur says in a recent book (*Finitude et Culpabilité*, Paris: Aubier, 1960) : "One may be astonished that the symbol has two usages, the one of which

red light signifies that I must stop: this is not a symbol, so much as a sign indicating something for my behavior. A word signifies a thing: it is not a symbol, so much as a representative sign for my thought. But a logical symbol does not refer to any particular content: it designates a structural scheme or a logical form that *governs* the legitimate procedures in reasoning.

A proper understanding of this may be gained simply by distinguishing between formalization and generalization. One might, however, at first sight confuse these two, since modern formalism gives rise to a much greater generality. For example, the universal quantifier gives to the universal proposition a wider and more general scope than did the ancient formulation. Likewise, the calculus of classes places the accent on extension rather than on comprehension. But Husserl warns us that the relation of subsumption between the formal and the material is not identical with the relation of subordination between the general and the particular. The formal is not a genus of which the material would be a species. Formalization, above all, makes its appeal to that power of abstraction which enables us to remove all intuitive content in order to shed light on the logical organization of discourse.

Thus take the concept of implication: there is no reference here to the essence of the terms or to a causal relation; the operator is defined completely by the truth table—that is to say, by a certain logical procedure applied to assertions of which one considers only the truth or falsity quite independently of the content. Similarly, with the concept of class: while classical logic hesitates between an interpretation of the concept in terms of

---

would seem to be the strict inverse of the other. Perhaps one would need to seek the reason for this in the structure of signification, which is at once a function of absence and a function of presence. It is a function of absence, since to signify is to signify vacuously or as a mere variable. But it is also a function of presence, since to signify is to signify 'something' and ultimately the world. Thus signification, in virtue of its very structure, makes possible, on the one hand, the complete domination and even creation of signs by the logician—for example the reduction of the sign to a mere 'character' and ultimately to an element in a calculus; and on the other hand, it makes possible the restoration of a full language, a language heavy with implied intentionalities and analogous references to other things, all of which the language somehow gives in enigmas."

extension ("Socrates is a man," that is, he belongs as an individual in the species "man") and an interpretation in terms
of comprehension ("Socrates is human," that is, humanity is
inherent in Socrates), modern logic definitely favors inclusion in
a class. The class is constituted directly by the grouping of individual beings, without reference to any specific property, unless it be to that of the attribution of the class to all its members. Of course, the class is itself defined by means of the
predicate: $X \in F = $ df. $f(X)$. But still, the predicate, in turn, is
interpreted in extension, as being simply the totality of individuals that verify the function. And this is understood to
mean that two functions are identical if they have the same range
and if for each of their arguments they have the same truth
value. In this way, formalization separates the form from the
content and specifies the formal property in terms of the
logical process with which it is bound up. This process is then
objectified, and the logical object comes to be conceived as simply a function of the process. Hence it would seem that we
might achieve a total mastery of this new language, of its lexicon
and of its syntax.

Another step in the same direction is accomplished when
logic submits to axiomatization. This operation is necessary because the ordinary calculus of propositions, so long as it sticks to
the method of truth functions, produces a mass of logical laws
that need to be ordered. Logic, indeed, desires to present itself
as a deductive system analogous to mathematics. And so it is that
the logician puts his cards on the table. As in the celebrated
example of *Principia Mathematica,* he defines his primary
terms, represented by their symbols, and the primary propositions or axioms. He then lays down precise rules for the formation and transformation of correct formulas. Given this much,
the logician can proceed to derive theorems, which, in their
turn, can be utilized to found new rules of inference. In this way,
the entire procedure is at once transparent and justified: the system thinks itself and, in a manner, presupposes itself. Moreover,
the pains that the logician takes in proceeding this way—for
example, the pains that *Principia Mathematica* takes in order to
define a law which in appearance is as evident as the principle of

identity—are not in vain. This is the root of that very clarity and security that one is able to gain only by abandoning ordinary language. If the principle of identity is now expressed by a double implication instead of by the traditional "A is A," this is because the verbal form "is" is very ambiguous. It functions as copula, and it also designates existence (and this is why, as Gilson has shown,[9] philosophical language has had to oppose *existere* to *esse*). But to take it merely as copula, one finds that it has, as Blanché has stressed,[10] very different usages. It can signify the inherence of an attribute in a subject ("Socrates is human"), the inclusion of an individual in a class ("Socrates is a man"), the implication of one attribute by another ("Scientists are learned"), the inclusion of one class in another ("Scientists are men"), an equivalence asserted now as a fact ("Paris is the capital of France") and now as a definition ("A circle is a locus of points equidistant from a center").

In symbolic logic these various meanings and uses are clearly distinguished, expressed by different symbols and manipulated according to different rules. It is no longer possible to consider as identical two syllogisms, the one having as its major premise "Men are mortal," and the other "Men are numerous." Instead, the copula is treated now as the sign of class inclusion ("The class of men is a subclass of the class of mortals"), now as the sign of class membership ("The class of men is a member of the class of numerous classes"). Moreover, it is made perfectly clear that the two relationships of class membership and class inclusion do not have the same formal properties. By such means logic can remain faithful to the Cartesian spirit: if we are attentive to the clarity of our ideas and to the legitimacy of our inferences, we can advance surely and rapidly.

And there is more, for security would in a sense seem to be automatically obtained. As Whitehead says, "By the aid of symbolism we can make transitions in reasoning almost mechanically by the eye, which otherwise would call into play the higher faculties of the brain."[11] This assertion deserves particular credit when we consider such things as calculating machines. For these realize, at least in part, the dream of a language which would think for us in a way that would be altogether infallible.

It is not a matter of chance if, in a two-valued logic, the symbols T and F can be replaced by I and O, which have an immediate application in electronics. Nor is it any cause for surprise that logicians have been called upon to construct such machines. Logic, in effect, operates in the realm of the analytic, and it develops implications that are necessary by virtue of certain previously admitted stipulations. Thus the behavior of a robot is determined by mechanisms that are themselves the expression of a logical necessity, that is to say, the analytic necessity of a formalism. Once a program is given, to put the logical procedure into operation is but the activity of a robot. Thus when Leibniz says, "Let us sit down and calculate," he is inviting us to have recourse to the automatism of logic. To be sure, we need Leibniz to invent the machine, as well as an engineer to do the programming for it. But once the rules have been stipulated and the program formulated, we can, so to speak, turn the meeting over to the robot. Indeed, we have every interest in doing so, once it becomes a matter of directing a bomb by remote control or firing on a plane in flight. Thus the elaboration of a logical formalism would seem to pay off, quite as much as does the construction of a calculating machine.

Nevertheless, there must still be a thinking being to appreciate the results. A calculating machine neither knows nor judges its own results. Even when it can check its own work, it still does not experience results as these are lived in man's experience. It runs, and nothing more. It has no sense either for the useful or for the true. That is why, if to think is to judge and to discern the true from the false or the good from the bad, one cannot say that the machine thinks in our stead. It merely functions in our service.

Logic and Truth

But what is the import of all this for logic? We are tempted to say that since formalization lends itself to mechanization, logic must function like a calculating machine and be indifferent to any such thing as truth. Going by this roundabout route, we would seem to have rejoined the nominalists in their conception of logic, a conception that was generally prevalent in logical positivism. Nominalism, in fact, conveys two ideas. First of all, it conveys a negative idea that constitutes, as it were, the background of nominalism's entire philosophic enterprise. This is the idea that thought can attain to no more than purely nominal essences. But in addition, nominalism conveys a positive idea. This is the idea that the meaning of a symbol is given by the syntactical rules according to which the symbol is to be used. These rules need to be stipulated, of course, but they depend entirely on free choice.

Nor does this amount to anything more than saying, once again, that logic is a specifically artificial language. And this, in turn, is to say no more than that logic is concerned only with the validity of discourse and not with its truth. For truth cannot be something arbitrary; it is not freely chosen by the mind; rather it is imposed on the mind by reality. In fact, the formula, "To each his own truth," which might well serve as a slogan for conventionalism, amounts to a downright countersense. To put the same thing in another way, we may simply declare outright that if logic is such a language, then logic is not a science. No doubt one can say, as people have been saying for a long time, that logic is a normative science. And yet the normative character of logic—in virtue of which rules are laid down to assure the validity of a piece of reasoning—certainly does not suffice to confer upon logic the characteristics of a science. After all, the rules as such are neither true nor false, unless one considers, as Aristotle did, that these rules only serve to make explicit certain ontological structures, a thing that nominalism absolutely refuses to do. And so it is, paradoxically, that if logic, considered as a normative science, is analogous to morals and ethics, it is precisely because in logic there are no morals!

Nevertheless, logic simply cannot accept any such radical nominalism,* involving as it does a complete indifference to

---

* Unfortunately, the word "nominalism" has many different senses and hence may give rise to serious misunderstandings. However, I am using it here in the way it is customarily employed by French logicians. In this sense,

truth. Instead, like any science, logic pretends to enunciate laws, which it is careful to distinguish from mere rules, since such rules are only means of arriving at laws and are themselves actually based on these laws. Moreover, such laws claim to be true. Why? The reason is that on the one hand, these laws have a bearing on the meaning and significance of the symbols and not just on their usage, as do the rules. Semantics, in other words, cannot be entirely subordinated to syntax. On the other hand, these laws claim to be true because they are not themselves purely arbitrary, after the manner of syntax. One therefore has to examine, apropos of these laws, first, what logical truth signifies within the field of logic itself, and second, what such truth signifies by reference to the world considered as extralogical. After all, a language can be more or less rigorous, but it is not true simply by itself; it is a means of saying what is true, that is, of speaking about the world.

For that matter, even validity itself cannot dispense with all reference to reality. For are not the terms "true" and "false" constantly being used in the logical calculus? Still, nominalism is not refuted merely by this fact. For these truth values that are assigned to propositional symbols are purely formal qualifications: they are determinations of form, not of content. Truth, in such cases, is not an adequation to reality, but a merely formal property that is invoked for the purpose of determining the validity of the logical operations, and not the reverse. What is more, these truth values can be relativized in the so-called multivalued calculi, once the principle of excluded middle has been abandoned. It is thus that the logician would seem to be able to decide freely on the degrees of certitude. (It should be noted, however, that this is not comparable to measuring degrees of probability. For this latter type of measure requires a definite, given content: for example, it is necessary that a die be given before one can possibly determine that the probability involved is one-sixth.)

---

it signifies a theory according to which a logical language is a language artificially elaborated. In such a view of language, the mind is considered to construct concepts, rather than to find them in experience; likewise, the mind interests itself in the syntactical role of such concepts, rather than in their semantic value.

Nevertheless, supposing the values T and F to have been assigned to propositions, when the logician proceeds to an evaluation, he discovers formulas that are true in all cases, and quite independently of the truth or falsity of the propositions contained in the formula. These tautologies are logical laws. Moreover, the aim of the calculus is to discern such laws; or, alternatively, the aim of the deduction is to derive such laws from among all the formulas that may be correctly formed within the language of a given formalism. What is the import of these laws? Are they true in the same way that propositional functions are true, merely arbitrarily and formally? Two questions present themselves here, as regards the truth of such laws.

First of all, are these laws arbitrary? What was held to be arbitrary to start with was the rule that one laid down at the beginning of the calculus in order to discover the law. But now it seems that the roles are reversed. It is the law, considered as a theoretical affirmation, which authorizes the rule, considered as a practical consequence. For example, it is the commutative law that authorizes the procedure of commutation. Or again it is the law of excluded middle that authorizes the following rule: given a proposition and its negation, if the one is false, it is legitimate to assume the other. Unfortunately, of course, not all the rules can be justified, for the reason that the deduction of the laws can be carried out only according to rules that have to be presupposed. This, indeed, is why every axiomatized system posits, alongside of the axioms that are themselves undemonstrated, certain fundamental rules such as the rules of substitution and the rule of detachment. Nevertheless, in most cases the reciprocity of the rules and the laws tends to lessen the arbitrary character of the rules.

The laws themselves are in no wise arbitrary, because they have a bearing not only on the operations, but on the meanings. Indeed, this critique of conventionalism has been well expressed by C. I. Lewis:

The use of linguistic symbols is indeed determined by convention and alterable at will. Also what classifications are to be made, and by what criteria, and how these classifications shall be represented, are matters of decision. Insistence on these facts is sound. Nevertheless such conventionalism would put the emphasis in the wrong place. Decisions as to what meanings shall be entertained, or how those attended to shall be represented, can in no wise affect the relations which these meanings themselves have or fail to have. Meanings are not equivalent because definitions are accepted: definitive statements are to be accepted because, or if, they equate expressions whose equivalence of intensional meaning is a fact. And rules for the manipulation of linguistic symbols, and the transformation and derivation of expressions, can indeed be made at will. But the meanings which our symbols represent cannot be manipulated at all.[12]

This entire reflection serves to remind us of our condition as thinking beings. When we think, we are free, and yet we are not free either. We are free to be logical or not. But once we have chosen to be logical, we are not free any longer. Or rather our liberty ceases then to be capricious; it consists, instead, in obeying the truth, and the truth imposes itself upon us in the light of evidence.

But just which truth? In a "logic of truth," as Husserl says, is not the truth simply an effect of a valid consequence? Just how are logical laws true? They seem to be analytic and true a priori. Universal and necessary, such truths—since they do not depend upon the truth of the elementary propositions that they bind together—are valid for every possible world, like the eternal verities of Leibniz. And yet however much they may be empty of all empirical content, they cannot be absolutely empty, for the very reason that they can claim the dignity of truths only if they are authentic assertions and not mere verbal forms, or if, to use the terminology of Wittgenstein, they are not *unsinnig* and if they preserve themselves from sheer nonsense. They must have some sort of meaning: if not a *Bedeutung,* which would involve a reference to an extrinsic content, more or less vague, then at least a *Sinn*.

However, nominalism is not checked by this difficulty: the meaning of such truths, the nominalist will say, refers to an object that is produced entirely by syntactical rules and guaranteed simply by the morphological self-correction of the formula. Such a purely formal being does not designate any reality, but only an intellectual operation. The logical object is the act of a thought that thematizes itself. And logic thus becomes the expression of such thought as is conscious of its decisions and its processes. It is knowledge, to be sure, but knowledge of itself.

Nevertheless, when nominalism proposes this interpretation of logic, it does not take it seriously, because such an interpretation would lead the nominalist both to an examination of those acts of consciousness that aim at a meaning, and to an examination of the evidence in which this meaning presents itself. Such an interpretation would have started nominalism along the same road that Husserl took in moving from formal logic to transcendental logic. However, in order that we may follow this same road ourselves, we must make a detour.

It is sense or meaning, we said, at which logic aims. Apophantic analysis, as Husserl called it, undertakes to elucidate the various categories of signification (concepts, propositions, subject forms, predicate forms, etc.) on the three levels on which they are located: the level of what may be called the pure morphology of judgment, that is to say, of judgment in general, insofar as it avoids nonsense; the level of the logic of noncontradiction, or of distinct and determinate judgments, insofar as these avoid countersense or contradiction—which is accomplished through a fixing of the rules of derivation; and the level of the logic of truth, or of clear judgment, in which the formal laws of possible truth are fixed. Note, however, that *Bedeutung* in this context does not have the meaning that it has for Wittgenstein, who wishes to distinguish it from *Sinn*. Instead, these categories of signification are still such as to abstract from every object: "we shall say that they *are* significations or modes of signification, not that they *have* a signification."[13]

But is it possible to avoid all reference to an object? If apophantic analysis limits itself to a consideration only of possible truth, does such truth have any meaning apart from effective truth? The idea suggested here, that logical semantics cannot remain purely formal, is going to be forced upon us in consequence of the very effort that syntax makes to formalize itself. This effort, as everyone knows, has led to a *rapprochement* between logic and mathematics. Logic has become a calculus, just as Leibniz wished it to be. The study of the syllogism has been transformed into a concern with various laws from the calculus of propositions and the calculus of predicates. Likewise, the study of principles has been transformed into mathematical reflection on the criteria of formalisms in general.

However, mathematics, which thus lends its formalism to logic, has an import that is not merely logical, but ontological as well. For classical mathematics defined itself according to its domain —number, space, motion. And even modern mathematics, where the abstraction involved in formalization is carried much further, does not cease to involve a reference to an object, that is an object in general. Thus mathematics is, as Husserl said, a formal ontology. And from this point on, formal apophantic is absorbed into formal ontology. The categories of meaning or signification have, henceforth, for their correlates categories of objects (for example, object, unity, plurality, relation, identity, equality, whole, set, etc.) . Likewise, the thing becomes the correlate of the concept, and the state of the thing the correlate of judgment. In this way, logical language, for all its effort to be purely formal, does not cease to have an object. Nevertheless, this object is still formal itself. It is not the reality of the world; it is the form of a possible world, of a world in general, defined in terms of the notions of one and many, of totality and unity. It is an object to which thought may be said to submit itself in order to attain truth, yet only because thought has produced such an object itself and is therefore completely the master of it. For this reason, truth may still be defined as an accord of thought with itself, when thought reflects upon itself.

But one cannot stop here. To do justice to logical truth, it does not suffice to define it entirely within the formal system. It must be referred to an external reality, which calls for the adequation of thought to reality, which gives to signification its full significance and permits one truly to distinguish "meaning-ful" from "meaning-less." "Just as, in the system of Kant, the metaphysical deduction—that is to say, the internal deduction—of mathematical concepts must, in order to be 'true,' complete itself in a transcendental deduction—that is to say, a deduction that is related to the possibility of physics—so likewise, the formal analytic of judgment, with Husserl, attains completion only in applying itself to possible objects, and to possible objects which this time are no longer merely formal, but are materially given as well."[14] This is why Husserl supplements his logic with a transcendental logic. But we are going to proceed to transcendental logic by a slightly different route.

Truth and Reality

In order to bestow upon logical truth its authentic character, it is necessary, paradoxically enough, to contest its apodictic character by evoking the many difficulties that a program of formalization encounters. And, in fact, we have assumed up to now that logic was completely autonomous and that logicians were able to have a complete mastery of the field of logic. But now we shall see how the entire enterprise of logic is brought face to face with what Ladrière calls "the internal limitations of formalisms." Very possibly, these limitations all proceed from the fact that the very boundaries of logic bring it into contact with that ultimate and irreducible reality that lies beyond these boundaries. As a result, it is impossible for the intuitive content of logic to be completely eliminated in the process of abstractive formalization.

Indeed, a formal system can never be finished and closed. The formalized language of the system always has to appeal to a metalanguage. It can justify itself only by calling itself into question. No doubt, in what Husserl calls the "theory of multiplicities," that is to say, domains of objects that are determined by the fact of being subject to a form of nomological theory, the formalisms themselves become, for this type of metamathematics, mathematical objects, which one can then treat of with "the lively freedom of theoretical research." Nevertheless, when such research poses what might be called global questions of confidence in regard to such a theory of multiplicities—for instance, questions of noncontradiction and saturation—then reflection discovers that the theory cannot properly be either isolated or dominated.

For example, Gödel's two celebrated theorems demonstrate in effect that the formalism of a generalized logic can give rise to formulas that cannot be derived or proved within the system. If the system is not self-contradictory, then it is perforce incomplete, and the noncontradiction in its turn cannot be guaranteed by the logical resources proper to the system. Indeed, that the system is not self-contradictory can be proved only if the system becomes an object for another system more complex, and this latter system in turn for another, and so on indefinitely. Similarly, a theorem of Church's demonstrates that it is impossible to decide by means of a simple calculus whether or not the schemas of a formalism are valid. Thus the apparatus of demonstration has shortcomings: "Thought in most cases finds it impossible to characterize a priori the separation that is envisaged between true formulas and formulas that are not, from among the totality of formulas that are specifiable by means of the resources of a given formalism."[15] In short, there are insoluble decision problems, simply because logico-mathematical existence bursts the boundaries of what can actually be effected within any given mathematical system.

If this inability to stay within bounds is attested to in theories that are richer than arithmetic, it is because in such cases logical thought is confronted with an infinite that is no longer merely potential, but actual. The nondenumerable reveals to such thought its power and its impotence alike. Ladrière shows most ingeniously that all demonstrations of the limitations of formalism rest on the more or less explicit intervention of the diagonal argument, invented by Cantor to show the impossibility of establishing a one-to-one correspondence between the set of integers and the set of real numbers between zero and one. Formal systems lend themselves to this sort of reasoning because their structure corresponds to the entire set of integers. This set possesses the remarkable property of being unable to be exhausted by an enumeration, of being in a way capable of indefinite extension, and of being unable, nonetheless, to lead us to an effective totalizing of all its elements.[16] So long as one remains within the sphere of the denumerable, one considers only the potential infinite and excludes any infinite totality. In the sequence of integers there is always a next, since the sequence is precisely characterized by the notion of a successor, starting from zero. Indeed, one can even speak of the object that comes next after the sequence of integers as being the type of order of that sequence.

Such is the fate of thought when it has to deal with integers. It always has the possibility of going still farther, as Malebranche said; nor can it ever attain that limit at which the system would be closed in upon itself. Thought can perfectly well aim at what is merely virtual; but "if it is possible to aim at what is virtual in the actual, it is never possible to lead the whole of what is virtual over into the sphere of actuality."[17]

This indefinite potentiality for what comes next, which is the stumbling block for all logical thematization, is something that Ladrière has very judiciously compared with the question regarding the horizon of perception. It is well known how Husserl insisted upon this notion of horizon, the elucidation of which always serves to check the temptation toward idealism. Perception is always at the same time both evident and inadequate, because any perceived object involves a double horizon, an inner and an outer: (1) an inner one, because the synthesis of identification that grasps the object through a multiplicity of aspects or appearances never permits these appearances to coincide completely with the object; and (2) an outer horizon, because the object always stands out against the background of the world. The spatio-temporal totality is never assignable; the horizon always recedes when we approach it. Logico-mathematical thought has the same experience[18] of a horizon, and this gives rise to the operations of constructive thought, as Husserl had already noted, when he spoke of the idea as an infinite task that aims at thematizing the infinite horizon of the *et cetera*, "*die Grundform des Und-so-weiter.*"[19] No sooner does thought pretend to abolish the horizon, and to exhaust the inexhaustible, than it runs up against the contradictions involved in the theory of sets. It is precisely then that thought has recourse to formalization and refuses to grant mathematical existence to any objects save those presented in a nonself-contradictory formalism.

The same destiny that befalls mathematical thinking symbolizes the condition of all thought. Its source lies in the movement of temporalization in consciousness itself. The living present is a present that is always running out, that is ever precarious, and that can never be expanded to take in the dimensions of the whole of experience. The impossibility of elaborating a system that discloses within itself the genesis of its own meaning and the significance that returns upon itself in the manner of Hegelian logic merely signifies the impossibility of ever establishing oneself with the eternity of the *"tota simul."* The complete and total object of mathematics would be the object of an *intuitus originarius,* capable of a total reflection upon itself. The distance that separates thought from its object can never be abolished, any more than the distance from oneself to oneself, which temporality never ceases to open up. Indeed, the spatial horizon is like a symbol for the temporal horizon, to which all consciousness is committed.

So it is, then, that formalism is itself committed to limitations. This presence of a horizon that is ever receding should warn us that the formal ultimately ends in the intuitive. It is the intuitive that is the place of indefinite potentialities, the inexhaustible that never ceases to haunt and to provoke constructive thought. It is that which never ceases both to satisfy thought and to disappoint it. It satisfies it because it is there, in intuition, that something is given to thought. It disappoints it, because thought does not have mastery over that which is given, in the way it has over that which is formalized. Intuition here puts thought in contact with what is beyond the formal. At the same time, this beyond is something that we find on this side of the formal as well. For this intuition, not being original, is a derivative intuition; it is none other than that sensible intuition of which the form, as Kant said, is time. This intuition, in short, is at the two poles of formalization. One can say that formalism ends in the intuitive simply because it is rooted in the intuitive to begin with.

For that matter, it seems that one scarcely needs to seek out the intuitive at such a far remove as the two poles of formalization. Indeed, one might suppose that intuition comes into play with respect to the elementary operations of logical calculus, insofar as these are certifiable by the method of the truth tables. This procedure carries out the operations that are posited by a given formula, in order to arrive at a result that is equivalent to that formula. Does not such a procedure involve reliance upon intuitive evidence?

Still, it is well known that such evidence is capable of being achieved only in a very limited sector of the calculus—for example in the calculus of propositions. In a more complex formalism such as the higher functional calculus, the truth-table method is no longer sufficient. In other words, logical thought cannot limit itself simply to those elementary constructions in which it seems to dominate its object completely and to "realize" it and bring it into being. Consequently, it cannot continue to rely solely upon the evidence supplied by intuition.

Bachelard has often shown with great force that the progress of scientific knowledge has been accomplished by challenging the evident and by complicating the simple. Thus thought, as it proceeds in the direction of ever greater formalization, develops by destroying the bridges that link it with the elementary calculi. Why? Because, basically, the evidence of which these calculi are the beneficiaries is ambiguous: the evidence of what is intuited is analogous to the evidence of what is perceived.

However, it is certainly true that logical thought, in order to sustain itself, must re-establish contact with intuition, much as Anteus had to touch the earth again. But intuition here is no longer purely logical. Rather it is an intuition that precedes logic. Thus is it not significant that when we learn logic, we need examples to start off with? To understand implication as purely logical inference, which avoids all reference to causal connection, I must say that two plus two equals four implies that Washington, D. C. is the capital of the U. S. To understand the difference between class and predicate, I need to bring into play syllogisms having as their respective premises, "Men are mortal" and "Men are numerous." If the concrete is merely the abstract rendered familiar by usage, then usage requires that at the outset the abstract be clarified by the concrete.

We therefore proceed to formal truth by way of material truth. It is well known how Husserl insisted on the role of examples in ideation: categorial intuition is an act that has a ground and basis, and that ground and basis is in sensible intuition.[20] For the true example is the one that is really exemplary; it sets forth the essence. Yet such an example becomes exemplary by virtue of the operation which idealizes it and which discovers the ideal in the fact. By itself, the example is in the beginning *faktisch*. It is the grasping of the concrete individual as *Urgegenstand*. Also when phenomenology becomes, as it were, an archaeology, when, in order to return to the source, phenomenology removes the cloak of ideas, as the *Krisis* says—ideas whose sedimented knowledge has progressively coated the world—then phenomenology discovers the *Lebenswelt*, "the world in which we have always lived," the soil on which all thought is built up. And when thought forgets its origin in intuition, it must still have recourse to imagination. The ideation that discovers the essence and recognizes the form as essence has recourse to eidetic variation, that is, to an imaginary manipulation of examples which permits one to discern the exact contours of a concept or an assertion. Facticity cannot be entirely eliminated, however freely such variation seems to play with it. To be sure, in such cases, the real that is given is no longer considered for itself; and yet it is still evoked by reason of being an example. By such means, ideation is able to reach pure essences, an a priori, as Husserl so often said. Formalism can conquer its autonomy, but it cannot renounce its origin in intuition. It is perhaps this theory of variation that C. I. Lewis is thinking of when he affirms, as White puts it, "that I need only make an experiment in imagination to find out whether all men are rational animals."[21] White then adds, "I do not find this early retreat to intuition satisfactory." And yet does a thought that wishes to be true have any other recourse?

Certainly, all this attests once more to the essential finitude of thinking consciousness. The formal systems which it erects are in a manner encased between two inexhaustible sources, the one prereflective, the other postreflective; the one the open horizon of logic, the other the open horizon of the perceived. Still, one can ask if these are not the same. For is not the truly inexhaustible source the world, now the world of formal ontology, now the *Lebenswelt?* And is not this the same world? The formal world is, indeed, but the form of the natural world, and thought, through its activity of formalization, attains to this only because it fulfills the wish of primitive intuition, being both summoned to the task and aided in it by the material world. Intuition is at the end of the process in the form of logical intuition simply because it is also at the beginning in the form of sensible intuition.

Moreover, the same thing can be said in terms of a theory of language. Linguistics distinguishes between syntactics and semantics. Syntactics treats of formation, that is to say, of the formation of discernible verbal forms or, in the case of logic, of correct formulas. Semantics treats of signification, that is to say, of the content that is designated by these forms. One may say with Granger[22] that syntactics and semantics are not located on the same level. Thus syntactics, which examines the organization of phonemes, refers back to semantics, which examines the meaning of the words. Also in its turn, the sort of syntactics that examines the organization of the words—that is, grammar in the traditional sense—refers back to the semantics which examines the meaning of the sentence or the discourse. In this way the study of signification refers to a stage of language other than the study of formation. Nevertheless, the ambition of logical language is to be sufficient unto itself and to find its semantics on the same level as its syntactics. This would be possible if the object that guarantees a significance to the formula were entirely expressed by the syntactical rules that govern the signs. However, this ambition is doomed to disappointment; every logical language is bound to have recourse to a meta-language, and this to a meta-meta-language, and so on ad infinitum. One may then very well ask if the authentic meta-language is not the common language, simply because this common language is, in fact, the only one in which the significance is immanent in the sign and in which the syntax, when it is not learned syntax—that is to say a phonological system—can set itself up on the same level as semantics.

Nevertheless, this conjunction is justified only if one introduces again a distinction between the language that speaks and the language that is spoken, a distinction that is analogous to that which linguistics sets up between language and speech. It is for the spoken language that the distinction in levels exists between syntax and semantics. This language is in effect language as seen by someone who has to learn it or to study it. It is a language that has become an object and is objectified in treatises on phonetics, in grammars, in lexicons. Hence it has become like a language that is strange to me, that I do not speak spontaneously, but which at every instant solicits my reflection.

In contrast, the language that speaks is the living and lived reality of the language, from which the language that is spoken is an abstraction. It is the same language, but one which is no longer dismembered and anatomized, and in which all the elements are united in the service of communication. Because I speak in order to say something to someone, the language that speaks speaks with me, and its virtue resides in its truthfulness, in its power to put both my interlocutor and me in connection with the world, a connection that is lived in a manner that is prereflective and prior to all logical control. In this life of language the signified and the signifying are no longer distinct.

Certainly, this common language risks leading us into error. And yet it can deceive us only because it installs us first of all in the truth. It can say what is false only because it can speak the truth. Indeed, it is to preserve us from such error that logic is constituted in the first place. But logic is not simply a system of precautions, a mere safeguard. If it elaborates a new language, more refined and more rigorous, it is still for the purpose of saying something and of saying it in truth. Nor is such a formalized language absolutely empty of all empirical content. It is at least, as Husserl says, an ideal object, that is to say, a product of ideation. And the ideation, which in this case is formalization, produces a form, and this form is a form of something. Now reality, or the world considered as the whole of reality, has forms and formal properties quite as much as it has a material body and empirical properties. The notions that logic treats of—notions such as those of "predicate," "class," and "relation"—designate aspects of reality or, as Husserl said, categories of objects. Nor are the syntactical rules purely arbitrary. They do not constitute the grammar of a mere game of chess, but the very texture of the real. Thus the rule of substitution signifies the identity of any given object whatever, considered simply with respect to its form. The formal laws are, therefore, objective laws and not mere operations of the mind.

Most assuredly, the object of logic needs to be constructed. There are artifices in logic, just as nominalism claims. But the empirical object likewise has to be constructed. To perceive is always to construct. There is no object for thought that is not an object of thought. Every object is the correlate of an intuition and is grasped by an intellectual activity. There is no other object of which we might be able to speak and which we might be able to know. But every construction has for its end to discover the given. It is because it keeps this contact with reality that logic is forever called upon to accomplish new feats and to achieve a perpetual progress. And if no formalism is capable of closure, it is because reality itself, considered in its formal aspects, is inexhaustible for a finite consciousness. Truth is truth only on condition of being always partial and provisional. However, the more or less obscure feeling for this inexhaustible character of the world is the resource of all creative thinking, provided only that such thinking never quit the shores of the world and that intuition not become "the dream of a visionary."

Such then is, roughly indicated, the sort of answer that we should like to give to the problem of transcendental deduction as posed by Kant. Just as mathematics is true because it gives rise to mathematical physics, so also logic is true because it gives rise to a mathematics with which, in the final analysis, logic becomes simply identified. And in becoming identified with mathematics, logic thereby eventually rejoins even physics. How is this possible? It is possible because logic has never totally burned the bridges linking it with the world and with the common language in which our first experience of the world expresses itself. For this reason, logic itself never ceases to speak of the world: logic is, indeed, formal ontology.

And with this we find that we join forces once more, if not with Aristotle, then at least with a modern logician who draws his inspiration from Aristotle. H. Veatch writes: "Mathematical logic is not really about logical forms at all, but rather about real forms and relations."[23] Such is, indeed, Husserl's notion too. For him, formal logic, considered as a "logic of truth," is an a priori theory of the object in general. To be sure, "formal" always stands in opposition to "material," and this is why Husserl reproaches Aristotle with having recognized only a general ontology, which he then took to be first philosophy itself. But he quite failed to recognize anything like a formal ontology. "The subordination of the material to the formal manifests itself in this, that formal ontology contains within itself at the same time the forms of all possible ontologies, with the result that it prescribes for such material ontologies a common, formal legislation."[24] This formal ontology is indeed a science, "the essential science of the object in general." And in this science the object in general is already an object, and the aspect of formality is a category of reality. Put a little differently, formal apophantic—the theory of predicative judgment—always has an ontological dimension. It seeks "to be the science of the possible categorial forms in which any object that might serve as a substrate must be able to exist, if it is to exist with truth."[25]

Now apophantic, as I see it, is almost the same as what Veatch means by "intentional logic." Accordingly, if we follow Husserl, we cannot accept any such radical distinction between mathematical logic and intentional logic as Veatch proposes. And yet I should like at this point to appeal to Veatch against his own theory. His philosophical perspective is that of realism: on the one hand, he discloses in a very ingenious way the affinity of logico-mathematics for the real; on the other hand, he affirms that "the nature and structure of the logical is determined entirely on the basis of its being adapted to disclose or signify the nature and structure of the real."[26] Hence, why erect such a wall of separation between an intentional logic, which would be an authentic logic, and mathematical logic, which, because it is a science of the real, would be a pseudo-logic? No doubt the distinction between formal signs and instrumental signs that Veatch insists upon is acceptable. But I prefer to say with Husserl that this gives rise to two orientations in logic, and without supposing that apophantic is to this extent radically different from ontology. After all, logic is always concerned with reality, and it finds in such a concern the justification for its pretension to truth.

Nevertheless, still another logic remains in fact possible and even necessary, if one should wish to examine somewhat more closely the interaction between logic and reality. This is transcendental logic. The notion of such a logic, as Husserl proposes it, has occasioned any number of debates. However, in asking ourselves how formal logic might be able to be true, and also in considering, albeit quite summarily, how formal logic is rooted in intuition and how it has recourse, at least implicitly, to common language, we have already ourselves become involved in this transcendental logic. For what is transcendental logic if not a reflection on formal logic and a reflection that is oriented toward the transcendental question: just how is such a logic possible?

To answer this question, it does not suffice to discover thought as somehow capable of achieving an a priori. It is necessary in addition to discover how this thought constitutes itself and functions. Even in the case of Kant, alongside the transcendental analytic, which enumerates the a priori elements in knowledge, we find the germ at least of an intentional analytic that describes the operation of the *Gemüt*. In short, transcendental logic ought to end in a phenomenology and in a genetics that would explore the sources of logical thought: "That which should be absolutely first in any theory of evident judgments (and therefore in a theory of judgment in general) is to trace back genetically the evidence that is predicative in form to the evidence that is not predicative. And such nonpredicative evidence is simply called experience."[27]

Experience is our first vital relation with the world, as this is lived in perception and named in speech. For speech is this original tie with the world, the world which is contemporary with perception and inseparable from it. The first consciousness that bears the logical consciousness is already a speaking consciousness. This is why the logical language is rooted in the natural language, just as formal thought is in intuition. Phenomenology, considered as transcendental logic, invites us, then, to return from the language that is spoken to the language that speaks, the language that is speaking because man speaks, but also because the world speaks to man, and this, in turn, because a veritable alliance has been sealed, even from birth, between man and the world. It is this phenomenology of living speech that we must now undertake to sketch out.

(3)
Language
& Metaphysics

OUR INVESTIGATIONS thus far have led us to the idea of a phenomenology of language. Still, we must not allow this concern to deflect us from our final goal, which is that of a metaphysics of language. And yet will not a phenomenology of language ultimately lead to such a metaphysics? It would surely seem so, since what such a phenomenology will tend to do is to show how, in language, is manifested that reciprocal tie which unites man to the world.

To begin with, however, phenomenology presents itself as a sort of psychology, a psychology without any physicalist presuppositions. Indeed, it was just such presuppositions that forced Husserl to insist upon the irreducibility of phenomenology to psychology, to denounce the temptation to psychologism, and to save himself from such temptation by the device of reduction. By neutralizing man's naïve belief in the reality of the world, yet without denying the world; by reducing the world to the phenomenon of the world, yet without contesting the reality of the world, Husserl assures to consciousness its transcendental status. And this is what is important in his eyes.

Still, phenomenology—especially when it assumes a more or less genetic character and seeks to trace formal logic back to a transcendental logic—invites us to consider the concrete human subject. Nor is this subject a pure form, like the Kantian transcendental subject, but rather a subject that is incarnate and temporal—a living person, in short. And yet the transcendental subject loses none of its rights for thus being concrete. On the contrary, it is the whole of the human person that is thereby promoted to the dignity of being a transcendental subject. This body which I am, this culture which I incarnate, this language which I speak are all constituents of this subject by the same title as the acts of consciousness themselves. My total "I," the psychophysical "I," say the *Méditations cartésiennes,* is engaged in an intentional relation with the world—not merely a relation of knowledge, but one of sentiment, of will, of action, as well. I am an absolute, but this absolute is relativized by being ever engaged in concrete relations with men and with things. For the reduction, far from neglecting these relations, on the contrary sets them in relief; far from abolishing the world, it discovers the world as the horizon of horizons. Hence it is inevitable that the metaphysical question par excellence should arise: What sort of being is man, if he is oriented toward the world and adapted to it? What sort of being is the world, if it is man's homeland? Is there not between man and the world a sort of pre-established harmony?

The interesting thing is that language provides us with a means of access to this problem. Or better, it is not language so much as the speaking relation that man has with the world. For we shall no longer consider language as an object of science, namely, of linguistics; or even as science itself, namely, logic. Our preceding reflections have invited us to turn our attention toward the ownership that language has of meaning and toward the usage that man makes of language—that is to say, toward man as speaking and toward language itself as speaking.

In truth, these two themes would seem to split the phenomenology of language in two, each part with its own proper direction and concern. For on the one hand, to consider the human being as a being who speaks tempts one to see in a language a tool, of which man is the master and which he can make over according to his taste, precisely as the logicians do. Consequently, one is tempted to affirm the primacy of thought over language and the arbitrary character of linguistic signs. But, on the other hand, to consider language as language that speaks tempts one to see in language a reality which both precedes and outruns thought, which instructs thought without thought's having any initiative whatever, and which proceeds not from man so much as from the world. If language is language that speaks on its own account, then it is the world that speaks and proclaims itself in and through language. Indeed, language itself is something natural and not artificial precisely insofar as its signs signify naturally.

Nevertheless, these two themes should be joined. For man speaks in order to communicate something, and he does so with signs that already have meaning and significance. Communication, considered as an activity of the human being as a speaking being, is different from conveying information, which is a character of the language as spoken. Communication conveys not only information, but meaning and significance as well. By language, man transmits meanings: he then communicates with others. But he also experiences these meanings: he then communicates with himself. And finally, he discovers these meanings: he then communicates with the world. And this is because it is essentially of the world that he speaks. Moreover, he can do this only if the world reveals itself to him, not simply as being there, but as being significant, as being able to be said. In other words, man can speak of the world only if the world speaks to him.

Language and Thought

Man speaking is man thinking. It is most difficult to define thought. And one recalls how Descartes, when asked what the meaning of the *cogito* was, replied that it is an evident notion requiring no further explanation. Nevertheless, we can conceive of thought as a phenomenon, in the sense of the word intended by phenomenology, that is to say, as a type of behavior that manifests and reveals its own proper meaning. From this it follows that it is speech which attests to thought: the *cogito* is a *loquor*, and intelligence is a certain manner of using language.

The objection that a thought can be silent and not articulate itself in words need not detain us, because even if thought can be
silent, it is not for that reason mute. The man who thinks communicates with himself in a silent monologue, and the monologue of the theatre is doubtless the least artificial element in a
dramatic presentation.

We are not pretending that thought is reduced simply to words.
But the spoken word is certainly a necessary condition of
thought. Of course, we can speak without thinking, just as par-
rots do when the emission of the sounds is but an immediate reaction to certain stimuli; and it is very possible that a large part
of our daily conversation is traceable to automatic responses and
emotional reactions. Still, we cannot think without speaking,
and the way in which we use language reveals the way in which
we think, and ultimately it is the measure of our intelligence.

The necessity for this recourse to language becomes apparent
if one defines thought, very summarily, as the manipulation of
representations, and if one then distinguishes representation
from presence. In our prereflective life, or better in our pre-
thinking life, the world is already present, much as the environment is to the animal. This *Umwelt* is already specified by our
sensorial structure, as well as by our needs and our aptitudes,
which even at this stage exercise a transcendental function. But
we are still entirely immersed in this world. Our relation to it is
an immediate integration in it, much as the infant's is to the
mother's breast. It is thus not a communication between relatively autonomous parties, as subject and object are. Independent thought starts as a result of a break: it is, indeed, by a sort of
original sin that we denounce the primordial pact that we have
with our milieu, a pact which Rilke honored so deeply in the
case of animal existence. And it is through such a break that we
lose paradise. Then it is that we separate ourselves off, so as to
say "I." The *cogito*, indeed, is an *ego cogito*. To become conscious of the world is also to become conscious of oneself as a
distinct pole of reference. To think requires this distance with
respect to the world, a distance that is expressed by the "re" in
representation. Nor is it surprising that, henceforth, reflection

should be constantly tempted by the legerdemain of idealism, according to which the world is no more than my representation of the world.

Now just how is this transition possible from a condition of mere living to one of thinking? It is possible by means of language. It is language that introduces the requisite distance between the signifying and the signified. It is by the mediation of language that the interval is created where thought can come into play. Nevertheless, we shall soon see that the mediation is one that separates and unites at the same time. If language digs a trench between the world and me, it also throws a bridge across it. The word inserts itself between the thing and me. But still, the word does not restore the actual presence of the thing, which has now become meaningful and significant.

On the other hand, at the same time that the word arouses thought, language assures thought of its vocation to be logical, to seek sense and meaning, and to search for it by following the thread of a logos, instead of merely wandering around at the whim of chance. For does not every language involve a minimum of logic? The mere linear sequence of symbols introduces an order into ideas; likewise, it gives the means for discovering and proscribing both nonsense and countersense. Even if common language is a deceiver, it nonetheless aims at rationality, and it never fails to subject thinking to a certain discipline.

At the same time that language permits thought, it also permits the consciousness of self. That is to say, it permits it by introducing this same interval, this thin film of nothingness, as Sartre called it, which separates me from myself and makes me into a *pour-soi*, a for-itself. Moreover, it does this by shattering the opaque identity that defines the *en-soi* or the in-itself. The "I" is another, Rimbaud said. This does not mean that I lose all control over myself, that I become a stranger to myself, as in cases of mental alienation. Quite the contrary: I become conscious of myself; I become intelligible at the same time as intelligent; and I become capable of universality. I was lost in the world, and in speaking, lo, I become what I am. My speech commits me. I am what I say, and every genuine word is a word of honor. Likewise, my speech reveals me to myself, just as it does to others: in communicating, I thereby become myself a communicable being.

Indeed, this unversality which speech confers upon me is in some way intermediate between the multiplicity of the ineffable singular and the formal identity of the transcendental ego. But if speech thus forms me and commits me, it is because at the same time I am not what I should be. I have always to be what I ought to be, and I can always not be what I ought to be. My identity resides in the fact that I do not identify myself with anything. It is an identity that is beyond all discourse, but it is discourse alone which can inform me of it, insofar as discourse reveals this self of self-consciousness which at one and the same time I am and am not. Thus language is necessary for the emergence both of consciousness as the power of representation and of self-consciousness as the power of affirming oneself in denying oneself. That is why, as we shall want to say and say again, man is always in the thick of language.

However, we can verify these effects of language by instituting a counterproof, that is, a proof that works from seemingly negative and contrary instances. There are men, for example, who do not have complete mastery of language. But these are still men nonetheless: a fool is a foolish man and not a normal animal; he continues to manifest his humanity in his very folly, for he still speaks. His difference from others does not bear on consciousness in general so much as it does on intelligence. But we can at least measure this difference on the basis of the man's way of using language. Goldstein has established, quite beyond doubt, that aphasia reveals an intellectual deficit.[1] It is an illness that in all its forms unsettles what Cassirer called "the fundamental symbolic relation." The word is no longer used as a sign, that is to say as a substitute for the object and as something introduced between subject and object. Rather in such cases is manifested an actual retrogression from the level of representation to the level of presence. Moreover, the patient's other attributes confirm the fact that he is no longer able to step back from the world, in order to consider it; instead, his behavior is reduced to "emotional attitudes" or to "concrete operations." This incapacity to abstract oneself from the immediately given, so as to schematize it and conceptualize it, is what Goldstein calls "the loss of the categorial attitude."

On the one hand, therefore, one notes that among aphasiacs there is a mutilation of intelligence, the various aspects of which Ombredanne sums up as follows:

"1. Sensibility to the concrete effects of situations, particularly to those which touch the patient's affectivity, together with a despotism of these effects.

"2. Difficulty in effecting the synthesis of concrete elements in the unity of a proposition, a difficulty that is all the greater insofar as the order in which these elements are presented needs to be broken up and replaced by another on the initiative of the subject.

"3. Instability of propositional groupings, and a necessity for returning constantly to the data of the problem.

"4. Difficulty with abstraction, which is tied up with a tendency to perceive differences rather than resemblances, and, among the differences, those that immediately touch the sensibility.

"5. Difficulty in making interpolations and extrapolations that are at the basis of inductive and analogical representations.

"6. Impossibility of utilizing in these operations symbolic schemas, formulas of simplification, algorithms.

"7. Substitution of a step-by-step approach for schematization.

"8. Poverty of invention, appearance of reproductive solutions in place of productive ones.

"9. Considerable limitation of educability due to the slowness of acquisitions, the fragility of the scaffolding of such acquisitions, and the omnipotence of conduct belonging to a lower level. Such conduct, by being substituted for conduct of a higher level, constitutes and entails errors, with frequent catastrophic reactions resulting.

"10. More generally, a slowness in all discursive processes and a marked tendency to fatigue."[2]

On the other hand and reciprocally, an intelligence that has thus deteriorated cannot make a normal use of language: one can verify this by examining the language of the aphasiac. One might study here the role played in this language by syntactical morphemes such as "thus," "therefore," and "because," which point up the logical procedure of discourse. Unquestionably, these morphemes are gravely compromised as a result of the illness, since the language is no longer controlled, as is the language of logic in the very highest degree.

Nevertheless, Goldstein has concentrated on the impact of illness upon words rather than on phrases, on the meanings themselves rather than on their connections. And that too is very instructive. The word, we said, loses its function as a sign, and two other features of the word immediately move into the foreground. First, "the stereotyped word," such as occurs in ready-made phrases. Here speech is reduced to so many automatic responses, from which almost all meaning is excluded. Language under such circumstances can still seem rich, but it retains no more than a vestige of the richness that it displayed before the illness. It is now a language without a soul, deprived of spontaneity and productivity.

The second feature of the word that comes to the fore is "the individual word," which adheres to the object like a proper name; and it does this to the point of actually becoming a part of the object. In such a case the word designates, without any generalization or formalization, the aspects of the object that are immediately perceived and that are felt or reacted to in concrete attitudes of a sort to which the patient succumbs to the exclusion of everything else. For example, a patient suffering from an amnesia of colors, who can no longer declare *in abstracto* the names of the colors or even place colored objects in a proper order, can say: "This is blood red or sky blue." Another who cannot name a knife can say: "This is an apple-peeler." Still another calls an old memorandum book a gypsy wagon. These metaphors express either the possible usage of the object (for example, apple-peeler) , or its immediately perceived physiognomy (for example, gypsy wagon) .

But what is one to make of all this? To judge by these metaphors, must one say that aphasiacs are poets without realizing it? For the poets—and we shall come back to this point—return to the sources of language, the place from which metaphors spring. They deliberately make themselves children in the presence of language. But for Goldstein, the precise significance of aphasia is that the malady attests a regression toward a more primitive attitude, a sort of linguistic infantilism. Nevertheless, such an idea calls for some comment. Infantilism, as a clinical symptom, exists among adults because one expects of adults that they will behave as adults; it does not exist among children for the reason that they cannot prevent themselves from being children. In other words, the trouble resides precisely in the fact of regression, because regression represents an easy solution for an individual who does not want to control his tensions or to face up to the problems that confront him. Regression is thus a kind of surrender or a giving up; likewise the return to childhood is not a new childhood, but a caricature of childhood.

Only for poets or for saints, perhaps, is it possible to rediscover what is authentic in childhood. And even they do this by means that are those of an adult. Also, the apparent similarity between the attitudes and languages of the aphasiac and the child must not be allowed to deceive us. For there is an essential difference between the two: children are on the way to acquiring what aphasiacs have already lost, that is, the categorial attitude that gives rise to representation and logical thought. Moreover, Goldstein himself stresses how much the language of the child displays spontaneity and invention. His awkwardness in the use of language springs rather from an excessive richness and an impatient ambition. The child has too much to say, and all the more so, as he is so close to the world. But his trouble is that he does not know how to say it.

Furthermore, it must not be forgotten that it is from the adult that the child receives language in the first place. Not only that, but it is on the adult that we must all rely in order to learn what language is. Likewise, it is equally the adult, namely the poet, who is able to restore for us the truth of the language of childhood. And no doubt it is this first form of language that Goldstein calls the individual word, that is, the word that adheres to the thing and that seems at once both to depict the thing and to conjure it up, rather than to serve merely as an arbitrary sign of it. We shall also see that metaphors are the things that reanimate this original power of words. They are the veritable Fountain of Youth from which language derives a new vigor.

In contrast, the metaphors of aphasiacs are not true metaphors, as are those of the poets—unless, of course, one wishes to say that those who are mad are not so mad as we think they are. For there is a strange affinity between genius and madness. Still, to the extent to which aphasiacs are mad, their metaphors are metaphors by default and not by excess. Such metaphors are proof only of the fact that their users do not have control of the resources of language. It is only by chance that such users invent; it is not by virtue of any intelligence.

In this sense, aphasia is but the most spectacular aspect of a malady that upsets all the relations that the patient has with his world. The relationship between the degradation of symbolic instruments and the more general deterioration of behavior is not one of succession or of causality, but of simultaneity and reciprocity. Moreover, this only serves to confirm the fact that between intelligence and speech, between thought and language, there is a complete and total solidarity. Traditional psychology, however, has obstinately insisted on posing the problem as to which one of these terms is prior.

Must one say then that this is a false problem? Perhaps. Still, we suspect we know the reason why the problem has been posed. It is once more traceable to the distinction, useful but dangerous, between a given language and speech. This distinction is certainly justified to the extent to which, as we have said, the common language pre-exists before the individual intelligence. The child finds before him a language that he has to learn. The student similarly finds himself in the presence of a foreign language to be mastered. Indeed, for every human being speaking the language that he already knows, this language, already constituted, that I have referred to as spoken language, is like a tool placed at his disposal by culture in order that he may express his thoughts. This aspect of language seems, therefore, to justify the distinction between thought and language, and to permit an answer to the problem of priority. The answer would seem to be that a language, insofar as it pre-exists, enjoys a chronological priority, while intelligence, on the other hand, enjoys a transcendental priority. After all, if the language is conceived of as being a tool, then it is necessary to admit a difference of level between this tool or object on the one hand and the subject who employs it on the other. Intelligence, then, would be external to language in the way in which any power that sets the ends and the means is external to the means. However, this interpretation is too simple: the *homo loquens* is not a *homo faber;* and language is not identifiable with a tool of just any sort. But these are two points that we must now undertake to examine somewhat more closely.

The Human Being as a Being Who Speaks

We are always tempted to consider speech as if it involved simply the manipulation of a tool. For have we not said that language is the very mediation between the "I" and the world which causes the world to appear as that which is not I, and which I am able to name? And is not the attribute of the tool to permit an efficacious activity, that is to say to give me a grasp of an object that I have at a distance? One knows how much Bergson was wont to insist on the vocation of intelligence as mastering objects by means of tools, as well as on the function of language as being somehow a privileged tool for the intelligence. But it is Bergson who refuses to let either intelligence, or language that serves the designs of intelligence, have the last word. Still, it is ironical that, in pushing his criticism, Bergson continues to speak and to discuss. Indeed, if he can thus use language against language, it may well be because in its origin language is really not a tool. At least, it is not a tool like other tools. And we can verify this fact, in that language has a way of thinking on its own account, whereas an ordinary tool is inert and signifies nothing, and exists as a tool only at the moment when one uses it. It is even fashioned in view of such use. Doubtless, nominalism would wish to say the same thing about language, at least to the extent to which logic elaborates and develops language. And yet we have seen that language in this sense escapes the logicians and poses problems which cannot be resolved with the resources of logic alone.

At the same time, it must be admitted that everyday speech

does use language as a tool. For it employs language in order to
communicate. Thus it would seem that language is not just a
mediation between the world and myself; it is also a mediation
between others and myself. And here indeed is an instance of a
use of language that can properly be called a normal use. Moreover, it is noteworthy that those who are considered abnormal
are precisely those who are no longer capable of such a use. Goldstein observes that aphasiacs are not interested in others, being
given rather to withdrawing in upon themselves in a closed
world. In short, to maltreat language and to be ignorant of
others come down to the same thing. And this, in turn, is but a
further proof of the fact that speech troubles are only one particular aspect of a trouble that disturbs the total behavior.

Perhaps, though, in what we call the normal forms of communication, it is still necessary to introduce a distinction. When
I address someone, it may be in order to inform him of something
by communicating a message to him, or it may be simply in order
to make him a witness to what I have to say. In such a case, when
I communicate, I put to the test the truth of what my words
mean and signify. I expect of the other that he sanction this
truth, or perhaps that he himself produce it on his own part.
Thus it is that the poem exists as an aesthetic object only when
it is read, or the painting only when someone looks at it. And
even scientific truth is established in its omnitemporality, as Husserl says, only through the consensus of human minds.

Finally, thought can also address someone in order to act
upon him, and then it is that language becomes in effect a mere
tool. Man has no other means of swaying the gods but through
his prayers. The child who does not speak has recourse to tears
or cries. Indeed, there is nothing that cannot be or become language in this perspective, inasmuch as here the sign has no other
function than to provoke a certain reaction, much as a signal
does. Thus the paradigm for language in this sense is the language of command—orders that are given for troop maneuvers,
or equally, instructions that are given in, say, skiing lessons, or
tennis lessons, or driving lessons. In such cases, the learner may
well be given detailed explanations, and yet the objective is
simply that he eventually come to be equipped with various re-

flexes: it is not a question of his understanding, but rather of his doing something. In other words, language as a tool has the effect of making another person do something, much as the plowshare turns the soil. Nor is there any denying the fact that many of our words aim only at eliciting more or less automatic responses: their end lies not in themselves, but in the actions that they set in motion. And this is why the gesture as a mere call to action is quite as effective as speech.

There is, however, a more subtle way of acting on others than through orders or prayers, and that is to awaken in the person a certain sentiment: instead of making him do something, making him feel something. Here again there are diverse ways of arousing a feeling: terror can be provoked by blows, as much as by threats. In any case, in order that the threats may have their effect, they must be uttered in a menacing tone: one's speech must become terrible in order that it may strike terror. And so it is that to arouse a feeling in someone else implies that I express a feeling myself, that I play on meanings which are no longer conceptual but emotional. Language then serves less to name an object than to express myself, or more exactly, what language consists in here are the signs that accompany speech and serve to redouble its meaning. One of the reasons that forces linguists to distinguish language from speech is the fact that speech always involves aspects that pertain to prosody—such things as accent and intonation, not to mention gestural commentary, all of which have nothing to do with the basic structures of language.

Philosophers of language, too, note this duality: "The difference between what is expressed and revealed, on the one hand, and what is presented and asserted as secondary conceptual content, is not always noticed, but must be emphasized,"[3] Frankena writes in a chapter in which he expresses the distinction between "the cognitive and noncognitive aspects of language." To be sure, the study of these noncognitive aspects of language can serve to confirm a behavioristic theory like that of Malinowski, for whom "language in its primitive function and original form has an essentially pragmatic character."[4] Thus if I express my grief or my desire, it is because I expect that others will respond to my feeling.

Still, what is of particular interest in such a study is not its tendency to confirm behaviorism so much as its disclosure of a fundamental and different mode of communication. For if I expect that others will respond to my feeling, it is because I believe that they will have understood the signs by means of which I express it. This sort of comprehension operates on a primary level of intersubjectivity that one can call emotional contact: such is the nature of the so-called "sympathy" that Scheler describes.

However, does one have to say that this primary form of communication is a primordial form? Does one have to say that men exchange ideas because they first share feelings? The subtle analyses of Scheler show that sympathy is a complex and ambiguous phenomenon. And so it is, too, with that silence in which a person's expression is read in his glance or in his gestures. For such silence can arise at a point that falls far short of articulate speech and on a level that involves little more than a kind of symbiosis that is still animal in character. (It is thus that the dog knows his master's anger.) But such silence can equally arise at a point lying beyond articulate speech and on a level that involves authentic communication, as in the case of two friends who understand one another with a minimum of words, or in the case of the communication between man and the world (for it is man alone and by himself who is able to read in the *Sonnenschein,* as Heidegger calls it, no less than the brilliance of being itself and the polemical identity of *einai* and *phainesthai*) .[5] In any case, what falls short of language, as well as what is beyond language, is conceivable only when one starts from language. Even the crudest emotion tends to speak out, even the most eloquent silence to be broken.

This recourse to language is significant. Language attests to man's vocation to thought and, above all, to intelligence. Malinowski refuses to accept such evidence when he writes: "To regard language as a means for the embodiment or expression of thought is to take a one-sided view of one of its most derivate and specialized functions."[6] But is it necessary to explain the superior by the inferior, to explain speech in terms of mere talk and chatter, and the language of words in terms of the language of gestures? As soon as man speaks, he renounces a merely emotional contact and makes an appeal to knowledge. And whatever may be the amount of the affective charge that certain words have, they also have conceptual content. Frankena has clearly noted this. One cannot distinguish once and for all the cognitive from the noncognitive. "Emotional significance is noncognitive in itself, but we must admit that it is cognitively founded." Likewise, Frankena quite rightly criticizes Parker's proposed interpretation of the sentence: "I love you." Parker maintains that this is in no wise a proposition but a "volitional expression, which seeks to share a desire or satisfaction, or to make a desire prevail . . . , the lover's love is a force there trying to kindle a like warmth in the beloved."[7] Certainly, the person who says "I love you" hopes to get some sort of response in return. But this is precisely because he conveys something that is to be understood and not just felt. To declare his love is not merely to say that he is in love; it is to reveal love itself by naming it. In the *Chartreuse de Parme,* one recalls how Count Mosca, meditating sadly on the flirtation he sees beginning between the Sanseverina, with whom he himself is secretly in love, and Fabrice, says to himself: "If the word 'love' comes to be uttered between them, I am lost." In other words, he is conscious of the real power of this word. Even to name the half-conscious feeling that the partners have for each other is to bring it to consciousness and thereby to set in motion an irreversible process. And the reason is that to name something discloses a veritable new world—acts and words and things all take on a different aspect. Nor is it otherwise when the word "freedom" comes to be pronounced by an oppressed people. Men are led by concepts more than by passions; they live and die for ideas. If love is impassioned, it is because it is conceived of as love. It is the concept that awakens and requires the passion. And the concept, in turn, presupposes the word. Even the language of gestures, which can be most eloquent and convincing in a love affair, derives its meaning from the language of words; so long as the words have not been spoken, it is all but a game or perhaps the action of an animal in heat. In short, the level of intersubjectivity before speech sets in is the prehuman level.

So it is, then, that language is the promise of reason. Its virtue consists in conferring objectivity on meanings and realizing through communication a veritable community, which is a community both of minds and of ends. If, besides, I express certain subjective contents, it is because the subjective can also be advanced to objectivity, because it offers a meaning that is communicable. Intelligibility is not a privilege enjoyed only by logical assertions. Logic, before becoming the science of formal systems that aim at pure rationality, is first of all the presence of logos which all genuine speech evokes and which unites human beings with one another. Intelligence is the consciousness of this logos and not the manipulation of a tool, because language is no longer a tool when it is used for genuine communication, that is to say, when it does not serve merely to make someone do something, but rather offers something to be known and understood.

On the other hand, the way in which human beings speak confirms the fact that language is not simply a tool which intelligence might fabricate for its own proper ends and over which it would then exercise a total control. In effect, when I speak, I am my speaking; I become one with my words. Certainly, as we have already said, to speak puts me at a certain distance from that of which I speak. But between my consciousness and my speech there is no distance at all: I am in union with the language I use. No doubt, it is much the same with a tool: the driver becomes one with his vehicle, just as the rider does with his horse. But it is in the same way, as Bacon would say, that man obeys nature in order to command it. Docility with respect to a tool is the means of assuring oneself of one's power over it. If the driver becomes one with his vehicle, it is in order to drive it where he wants to go. But when I speak, is it a situation in which I may be said to be going simply where I want to? Does my intelligence even retain the initiative and control?

Yes and no. That depends on the intention that animates me. I can start talking without having anything to say, or at least anything that is premeditated or that calls reflection into play. Speech, then, is an exchange of signs and not of meanings. The formulas of politeness are exchanged much like figures in a verbal ballet. Even when speech is a vehicle for conveying information, it can be emitted in a completely unreflecting fashion. When one asks me the date of my birth, I may answer automatically (and in such a case even a lie can be automatic, if it is a pretty woman who gives the answer). If the words give rise to any reflection, it is rather on the part of my interlocutor, who, realizing my age, can comment on my response and can say, for example: "If you are so old, there's scarcely any hope that you will improve your intellectual performances." No doubt, I could myself anticipate such a comment, if the turn of the conversation should let it be foreseen, but the mental context here would remain vague since it was not explicitly translated into words. Thus speech can be without thought, just as emotional contact that stops short of speech is without thought.

But what happens when I have the intention of expressing an idea that is not already poured into a ready-made verbal form? I hesitate; I search for the proper words; I begin again. It may be that I stammer, or, on the contrary, that I speak too much, as certain orators do. In effect, I must both entrust myself to language and not entrust myself to it. It is not to any exercise in translation that I devote myself, as if I had to adjust an already formed thought to such words as were at my disposal. What is it that I want to say exactly? I am not sure of what I am thinking until I have said it, and I am not sure of what I have said unless I confront my utterance with what I am thinking: my wording puts my thinking to the test; and my thinking puts my wording to the test. A paradoxical situation, surely—one which can no longer be compared with that of the artisan confronted with his tool, but rather with that of the artisan confronted with the work to be done. For in this case the work to be done is indistinguishable from the tool, the project from the means for its execution.

A painter, too, has something to say, not with words, to be sure, but with colors. Does he know what it is? Look at him at work: he traces lines; he puts on a touch of color; and he contemplates his sketch. Then a new touch, a new examination. This hesitant behavior is not exactly trial and error. Each new feature, each coat, is commanded by those that have preceded, even if the painter erases them and corrects them. And on the other hand, each is examined and assessed in the light of a certain idea or a certain requirement, which the creator carries within himself, and to such an extent that the moment will come when he will say: "I've done it. It's finished." The real object and the ideal object then coincide.

Still, what was this ideal object that served him both as a prod and as a model during all the steps in the creative process? So long as he had not realized his ideal, he did not know what it was. The same dialectic is operative between the idea and the spoken word as between the project and the work, but the game is more rapid in the former than in the latter. The intention that is supposed to mean or signify something, as Husserl said, is empty until speech fills it in. Moreover, this intention is known only when it is realized. Oftentimes it happens that the realization appears maladroit: the words have betrayed me; I did not say what I meant. This is why poets and philosophers do not cease to speak, even after they have achieved what they know to be a peculiarly felicitous expression, much as the painter recommences with one canvas after the other.

Thought reveals itself in this very disquietude. And in this sense one can certainly say that intelligence commands speech. But it does not command it from above, in the manner in which art uses its tools. For thought does not even know or recognize itself outside of the language that both fixes and arouses it. Like the stroke of the painter, thought is a mixture of spontaneity and reflection: it precedes itself in the words that it finds; it is itself reflected in these words. Indeed, reflection is this return of thought to speech. Auguste Comte, even before Heidegger, made the observation that words are always richer in meaning than we believe, and that a wisdom as old as humankind is deposited in them. In this sense philosophy is always philology.

In this connection, it may be noted that Heidegger gives a privileged place to Greek (and to German), because he knows Greek so well, and also, it must be said, because the passage from Greek to Latin does attest a decadence in thought and culture. But if the linguists were more attentive to semantics, perhaps those who know certain archaic languages well would be able to discover in them analogous treasures. I cannot myself venture onto this terrain. What is more, it is not a question of contesting that it is to the miracle of Greece that we owe what is unique in the Occident; nor is it a question of discussing the diversity of languages. But whatever this diversity may be, the situation of human thought in relation to language is everywhere the same. Language is, if you wish, a tool, but it is a tool that thinks on its own account. Moreover, it is this character of language that I should now like to stress.

Language as Thinking

Let us then return to language as already constituted and as something that human speech simply finds at its disposal. To speak is to reactivate the intention that is hidden in the language. And the reason this is possible is that there is meaning and significance attached to the signs of a language. Indeed, this is why we have been able to speak of a *Weltanschauung* proper to each culture and proposed by each tongue.

But let us be more precise: it is necessary to consider first of all the structure of the language, the elementary syntactical forms which are common to the Occidental languages, and regarding which one can even ask (although it is up to the linguist to decide the question) if they are not common to every language. Moreover, when any such general structure of language is considered, it is properly intelligence that manifests itself, since intelligence is able to elaborate concepts and to explicate them in predicative judgments. A philosophy of language ought thus to begin with intellectualism.

But just which intelligence is manifested here? Not the intelligence of such and such an individual, who happens to speak and use the language, but an impersonal intelligence, which awakens the individual and directs him into the way of intelligence. I should like to cite here the analysis of Pradines,[8] because this analysis has not had the audience which it seems to me that it deserves, and because it is in accord, although seemingly quite by accident, with the criticism that modern logic makes of inherence. For Pradines's analysis suggests that the modern procedure in respect to the logic of predicates is but a refined expression of the spontaneous processes of the common language. Besides, it will be remembered that we ourselves undertook to verify the fact that between the natural language and the artificial language of formal systems the distinction is not so great, but that the latter remains rooted in the former and even finds that the natural language is an irreducible meta-language for any artificial language.

There is—at least in the Indo-European languages, Pradines says—a fundamental structure, which is that of the relation between a subject and predicate or verb. Pradines shows that this relation should not be interpreted as the attribution of a predicate to a subject, but as the attribution of a subject to a predicate. Only the predicate is given in experience, while the subject is constructed by thought as being implicit in the predicate. This thesis becomes clear if one considers that the first words in any language are the verbs. Accordingly, the first operation consists, so to speak, in substantifying these verbs. In French, "tonner" gives birth to "le tonner," and so to "le tonnerre." And I believe that one could note the same phenomenon in English, because English gives a privileged status to the verb as being the more original form, for example in expressions like "to hum" or "to pooh-pooh." It also utilizes verbal nouns and permits one to say to a friend who talks too much, "I'll do the talking myself"; or to a back seat driver, "Let me do the driving."

The next step, then, consists in attributing to the verb the substantive that has issued from the verb. For example, one considers that it is the thunder which thunders. The verb, in other words, calls for a subject. This appears clearly in the case of impersonal verbs. We do not say "Rain" or "There is rain," but "It rains," *"Es regnet," "Il pleut."* Naturally, to the extent to which the process of substantification is pursued in a given language, the dependence of the nouns on the verbs becomes less and less apparent. When we say, "The sky is blue," the substantive is altogether different from the predicate. Still, even this predicate is capable of substantification, since we do speak of the blue of the sky.

What, then, does this substantification of the predicate signify? It signifies simply the effort of thought to transcend the immediately given: a thing such as the blue over my head or an event like a clap of thunder are in themselves without significance; but they become acts that recur and are reproduced, as if they somehow bore witness to an energy or a permanent power from which such acts proceed. The thundering becomes the astonishing power to which one pays homage as to a god; the blue becomes the radiant power that the poets celebrate.

And next, what may we suppose the construction of the nominal sentence signifies? The noun designates the agent that is capable of the act and the nominal sentence refers this act to that agent. In this way, Pradines says, the relation of the subject to the predicate is basically a causal relation. The predicate finds in the subject the principle of its production and the foundation of its reality. Language, in other words, is penetrated by rationality. Undoubtedly, it can happen that this causality is sometimes travestied in the form of a mere animism. But must one say, as Max Müller does, that animism is a malady of language and hence of thought? I do not think so. It is at the very most a crisis of growth, for it represents the first and still very naïve expression of a dynamism that ultimately gives the principle of causality its full meaning.

Accordingly, in this language, the thunder thunders, just as pinks are pink, and the rapids are rapid. These phrases are no more tautologies than are descriptive propositions such as "Cape Town is the name of Cape Town." They are already synthetic propositions that set forth a causal relation. When I say, "Pinks are pink," or, if the denomination of the subject has freed itself from the predicate, "The sky is blue," I suppose that there is something in the flower or the sky which explains the pink color or the blue, much as a cause explains an effect. I am already tracing a program for a physics, a program that physics will accomplish with much greater success perhaps than biology, when the latter seeks to explain why, according to the famous premise, man is mortal. The subject is, in effect, the thing that is the cause. In French, the same word designates the two terms: *chose,* or thing, simply is *cause,* or cause. Further, in all these cases, the fundamental linguistic relation expresses a causal relation and not a relation of inherence like a mode of a substance.

In the light of such considerations, then, Pradines frees language from the charge that it involves a fallacious ontological commitment. The substantive does not designate a substance, whose essence we could know independently of this predicate. Instead, it merely gives a substantial reality to a phenomenon of experience expressed by the predicate. And it does so by founding it on the principle of causality: "All the relations that are involved in language can be traced back to those relations of cause to effect or of effect to cause which have appeared to us to be the type of every intelligible relation in the chain of experience."[9] And this certainly attests to the fact that an intelligence is at work in language. For if the subject is a predicate that is realized, then the predicate is a subject that is thought. As soon as the predicate is linked with the subject, the predicate is no longer felt, it is thought. To construct the subject is the same thing as to think the predicate. And this thinking is already a logical thinking, since it brings into play the principle of causality.

But we must now leave Pradines and carry our search for the evidences of thought and intelligence in language one step farther back. For prior to that promise of rationality that is inscribed in the very structure of language, it is possible to find a still more rudimentary manifestation of thought in language. Thus, is it not necessary that that very intelligence which manifests itself in linguistic structures be an intelligence that is exercised with respect to a given object? It is just such an object that gives rise to the questions for which intelligence tries to find the answers. But this requires that the object first be represented to me and that I be sensible of its presence, rather than that I simply be present to it, much as a man who is asleep, and as if I were but one object among others. In other words, consciousness is no less than that very light which makes the object appear: a veil is rent in twain; the darkness of the in-itself is dissipated; the world is revealed. Henceforth, I can say, "There is something." But what? I do not yet know. After all, appearances can be deceptive and confused, and it is necessary that I learn to explore them and decipher them so that their objective significations can be constituted. But what is essential is that the image arise and attest to the presence of something to me. This is why Kant said, in the first edition of the *Critique*, that the imagination is the common root both of intuition and of the concept.[10]

This emergence certainly requires both man's presence and man's initiative. It presupposes speech, as we have already suggested. It is when I name the object that there is created that space between the object and myself within which the object can appear before me. This is why man will not cease to be astonished before this ultimate why of human speech, and will sometimes claim for speech privileges analogous to those of the creator. Certainly, the word does not produce the object. But it snatches it out of the darkness. It conjures up its presence by a sort of spontaneous magic. To evoke something by naming it is to make it present. The ceremonies in which people appeal to the dead only repeat the rites that Ulysses and Aeneas practiced. The distinction between the imaginary and the real is not so great, so long as our day-by-day behavior does not enter in to accentuate the distinction and to make us feel the weight and the resistance of hard and harsh realities.

Right here we are at the moment of incantation, where it seems as if the word compelled the presence of the thing. Thus consider the famous, yet quite untranslatable, sentence from Mallarmé: "Je dis: une fleur, et, hors de l'oubli où ma voix relègue aucun contour, en tant que quelque chose d'autre que les calices sus, musicalement se lève, idée même et suave, l'absente de tous bouquets."[11] After this will be joined what Heidegger calls the struggle between the world and the earth,[12] between *Physis* and *Gaia*. It is then that there will be revealed the essential otherness of the real, its hardness, its opacity, the resistance that it opposes to both hands and concepts. And the qualities of what is present can manifest themselves only in this presence, and the presence is attested to by the image, and the evocation of the image supposes the human voice, the word that convokes the day: the world opens only at the Open Sesame of speech.

Nevertheless, this power is exercised by the word only because the world confers such a power upon it. If the imaginary can create the illusion of reality, it is because the world presents it-self first of all in images. But the important thing is that these images are already significant, and in such a way that with them presence is already meaning. This may be understood in several ways, for the nature of the image is ambiguous. Thus the images that gravitate around perception and, so to speak, provide a commentary upon it enrich the meaning of the object perceived; and in so doing they can be clearly distinguished from the im-ages in dreams, which serve only to hold a fascinated conscious-ness in thrall. Indeed, the imaginary is not always the unreal; or more exactly, the unreal is not always aberrant and alienating. It can well be a means of aiming at the real, and of fulfilling those empty intentions that animate perception. In such cases, rather than the unreal, it is a question of the prereal, that is, of a con-stant anticipation of the real without which the real would be but a spectacle without spatial or temporal thickness.

But one must go further. Alongside these images that heighten perception, one must make room for perception itself. And per-ception is still nothing but images. Yet the images this time do not maim or wound the real in the places where it is vulnerable; nor do they shatter it, so that the real becomes unreality. No, the real is simply snatched from out of the night of the in-itself. It comes into being for us, without being by us. In some way or other it itself calls itself forth. If Ulysses can conjure up dead heroes, or Mallarmé the flower, it is because the great abyss itself, or the springtime, being the potent images they are, invite them to do so.

This is as much as to say that the world in its turn speaks to us, and that in inventing language we only take steps to reply to it. For the images that it offers us are significant. And yet their meaning does not involve any "knowledge about," as Russell would say. On the contrary, the sort of sense and meaning that is involved in any "knowledge about" is conferred upon images by virtue of the kind of empirical reflection that is associated with science and technology. In contrast, the meaning that is proper to the images which the world offers us is an immanent sense and meaning, a "knowledge in," as one might say, through which the world announces itself as a totality.

In this connection, think of those grand yet very simple images like the sea, the earth, the mountain, the sky, the forest. What is the sea here, if not the great abyss, bottomless and turbulent? It is that very deep which, with "the wintry waves" that it creates, "unceasingly tears open its own depths and unceasingly flings itself into them."[13] And as for the earth, it is that which "without effort and fatigue, from out of the superior tranquillity of great riches, produces and bestows the inexhaustible treasure that surpasses all zeal."[14] However, when Heidegger comments in this way on a passage from Sophocles, he adds: "The first strophe names the sea and the earth, each of them overpowering (*deinon*) in its way. It does not speak of them in the manner of us moderns who experience them as mere geographical and geological phenomena and then, as though by an afterthought, brush them over with a few faint and fleeting emotions."[15] Indeed, before this modern meaning that is ascribed to natural phenomena could even arise, it is necessary that there first have occurred that mutation, and even that decline, which is involved when thought passes from the ontological to the ontic.

But why this mutation? Why refuse to grant that nature is for Sophocles also what it already is for us, and that it can still be for us what it was for Sophocles? If the perception that inspires Sophocles is true, it is so with all of its richness; it is as if it held the whole of science in reserve; nor must the covering ideas with which such perception clothes itself be despised by the scholars and archaeologists who remove the covering. M. Simondon exhibits this very well in the light of another example, that of the mountain peak. For primitive thought, given as it is to magic, the world is a network of privileged points: the peak is then "the lord of the mountain, which drains into itself all the force and efficacy of the region which it determines and dominates." And even today the Alpinists who climb this peak are moved by this same feeling. Indeed, modern science justifies the feeling: the peak is really the lord of the mountain because "it is toward it that are oriented the geological folds, as well as the earth's thrust which raised the entire mass."[16]

In any case, these grand images are, as it were, the high spots, the key points, in which the world seems to gather itself up.

These are in no wise forms that stand out against a background, but rather forms that carry in themselves the background. They are forms of such richness and plenitude as actually to constitute a face of the world, rather than to be merely one shape among others within the world. Moreover, that original and primordial thought which grasps such forms, that magical thought which creative thought in the arts will somehow relay, is of such kind as to keep in communication with the ultimate ground and source, the *Grund*, as Schelling called it.

However, there are multiple analyses that converge here. Quite as much as Schelling, we ourselves might evoke the modern mythologies in our effort to return to the origins, which is precisely what phenomenology is supposed to accomplish. M. Éliade, for example, describes those images which are symbols and which the myths serve to explicate. "The heavens directly reveal their transcendence, their force, and their sacral character. They exist because they are exalted, infinite, immutable, powerful." Thus, prior to all accretions in the way of myths and fables, prior to all valuations of a religious sort, "The symbolism is an immediate datum of the total consciousness, that is to say of the human being who discovers himself as such, who takes cognizance of his position in the universe."[17]

These images are at the same time feelings. Their very polyvalence, if we may call it that, is traceable to the fact that the human being is in such cases still immersed in the world, very close to the basis and ground. These are not images that are held at a distance, in the manner of a clear and well-ordered spectacle. They are rather preimages. They hold in reserve not just the possibility of a clear representation or a rigorous manipulation that science will exploit, but equally the possibility of a veritable delirium of fabling, where knowledge has gone completely astray.

On this level of what we have called preimages, the human being feels rather than sees. But there already is, and there always is, an intentionality in feeling: feeling is not irremediably alienated in its own subjectivity.* What the human being feels is

---

* Feeling nevertheless remains subject to a psychoanalysis—and along with feeling the myths in which that feeling expresses itself. And yet it must be a psychoanalysis in the manner of Binswanger, that is, a psychoanalysis of

that which touches him, that which speaks to him. But even this prefigures a certain face of the world and contains a world in potency. The sky is first of all the heavenly, and the heavenly reveals itself through the feeling of majesty or serenity. The image of the sky is already a first crystallization of this primordial experience. Let us listen to what Clémence Ramnoux, commenting on Greek mythology, has to say of the earth, Gaia:

Buried far deeper than the gods of the underworld, beneath the harvests that cover the earth with their tresses, farther submerged in the depths of memory than even the beloved image of the nurse, there reigns the Porteress, the basis of security and the reservoir of benefits. At the very bottom, where Gaia dwells, is the region of light and shadows. Gaia is not a personification, as people say, of the cosmic phenomenon of earth or of the human phenomenon of motherhood. It takes shape far beneath the depths of the earth and long before anything like the face of the mother emerges. No doubt, it is mere emotive potential in its pure state, which has been put into words. The names do not designate exactly either thing or person. They are names! Nothing but names, but sacred names.[18]

One sees here that the language by which the world announces itself is already present, contemporary with feeling. Feeling expresses itself in words at the same time that it crystallizes itself in images. I have said preimages, because these coarse images of a world do not yet limn distinct and identifiable objects. It is because they are in a certain way polyvalent that there are made possible the correspondences and the metaphors of which poetry is so prodigal.* When Baudelaire writes, "You are a beautiful autumn sky, clear and rose-colored," the identification that he

_____

Dasein in which the manifestations of the unconscious do not disclose only the avatars of an interiority shut in upon itself, but also the ties with the world in which human existence is engaged and the feelings of world that human existence experiences.

* At least when one considers the metaphors before they have become standardized and hackneyed. As Paul Henle has well said, "Metaphors, like chemical elements, display unusual powers in a nascent state." This is why, perhaps, it is not enough to say that "their function in general is to extend language" (*Language, Thought and Culture*, pp. 195–196). They are rather the very substance of language, considered in its origins, or at least in what we may suspect are its origins.

suggests is in no sense conceptual. The identification operates by grace of the feeling that is awakened both by the autumn sky and by the young woman, or rather that can at the same time be explained by the image of an autumn sky and of a certain young woman. In this way feeling excites poetic language as well as the language of myth.

Indeed, there is no mistaking the close alliance between myth and poetry. To consider only the example of the Greeks, Clémence Ramnoux observes that "according to the most plausible view, speculation in regard to cosmogony developed through means proper to itself, with its own characteristic register, and through the use of associative procedures which cannot be compared with the procedure of discourse, but which are none-the-less strictly regulated by a sense of symmetry and measure."[19] Myth is not objective knowledge. It is essentially the free development, in a consciousness that speaks, of the images in which feeling can be crystallized. This is why Kérényi calls these images mythologemes, in a book in which he analyzes at considerable length the example of the young girl and the young boy. So also Jung, for his part, calls them archetypes and shows with what great caution one needs to treat them if one is to understand them. For, as he says, these are "revelations of the preconscious soul and as such have a vital significance." Indeed, a faulty explication of them can even provoke a psychic lesion. And Jung adds, "I must entirely agree with Kérényi when he says that it is the world itself which speaks by means of the symbol."[20]

This is the essential point: the world speaks to us; it comes and lets itself be caught in the snare of words; the words that these grand images wrench from us are full of its presence. And here perhaps we are at the very source that we sought to regain, at that point where the world reveals itself to us, where what is spoken is itself speaking. This communication of consciousness with the world is precisely the thing which, according to Husserl, or at least according to certain of his interpreters, transcendental logic seeks to explore.

Nevertheless, we must here make one point quite precise in order to avoid possible misunderstanding: communication is not unity. Thus people sometimes present mythical discourse as witnessing to a certain unity between the primitive consciousness and the world. But if (and I say "if" advisedly) this unity has a meaning, it can be located only in what Schelling calls a proto-history, something of which we know nothing. Not only that, but it is also something of which there is nothing to be known, because a consciousness that was one with the world would be a consciousness totally lost in the world. It would be as blind and as mute as a stone. Now myth and poetry are discourse. As soon as man speaks, he is separated. If myth or poetry betoken unity (and the fact is that they betoken separation and falling away and distress quite as much), then it can only be that the unity is no longer a lived unity. As Ricoeur has well said, primitive man is already man split off and separated.

On the other hand, if language manifests this rupture through which subjectivity is constituted, it presupposes always the possibility of a communication. And it then raises the metaphysical problem of an affinity or an alliance between man and the world. For the grasping of the meaning which the world sets forth in images supposes that man is adapted to this meaning. To understand this language, to speak it in turn, man must be of the same race as the world, although it is not for me to develop this theme here.[21] For the present it suffices that we should have circumscribed the birthplace of natural language, that is to say, of the language on which the artificial languages of prose and logic are based.

After all, natural language is not the pseudo-language by which the individual expresses himself, as is the language of gestures, cries, or tears. These latter signs are still signals that provoke not thought but action. In addition, they express only the superficial "I," as Bergson would say. Or again, when one says of an artist that he expresses himself, that is a very different matter: the less expressive his language—that is to say, the more reticent, more discreet, more impersonal—the better he expresses himself. The less he speaks of himself, the more he reveals of himself. Of what does he speak then? He speaks of the world; and we learn to know him in terms of the world which he talks about, and which is one possible type of world among others. Accordingly, natural language is neither organized by intelligence nor animated by feelings. It does not express man's nature, but Nature itself. To speak is primarily to let the world speak for itself, as if it were speaking for itself through the poets: the voice of the poet is not his own voice but a Pythic voice, "the voice of the waves and the woods," as Valéry says. And without doubt, the poet must vibrate and resound to this presence. Indeed, the poet is wholly and entirely feeling, but this feeling is light and illumination as soon as the emotive potential is put into words.

Such, then, is what we may call the natural language: poetry. Poetry is the original language, language considered as true. Nor am I doing more here than simply saying over again what linguists like Jespersen have said, and philosophers like Schelling, Croce, and Heidegger. This language is true because it carries a meaning that cannot be said otherwise; it is the world itself that speaks. In this sense, and independently of all the motivations that linguistics will be able to discover, signs are not arbitrary, not even if they differ from one language to another.

They will become arbitrary, however, in proportion as they make themselves instruments of a rationality that waxes ever more demanding. For if the itinerary, which Husserl indicated to us as being one that passes from the formal to the transcendental, has led us from the spoken language to the language that speaks, and from prose to poetry, then it is surely necessary to return from poetry, where feeling expresses itself, to prose, where intelligence comes into play. However, I do not feel that one ought to put as great a distance between the two as Heidegger does. When language becomes more abstract and more reflective, when it becomes formalized, it always preserves something of its origin. One grasps this kinship and this continuity in the Greek texts themselves. The words that name the great images—the abyss, night, sky, earth—are at the same time names of gods, all inextricably mixed and mingled in cosmogonies and theogonies. Then next there appear names of different powers— death, passion, war—which still designate something divine. And finally, there emerge the concepts of ontology and physics, as a result of a sort of secularizing of the names of powers. But philosophy is already potentially present in cosmogony: "Profound ontological speculations are set down in the verses of Hesiod;

and yet he would never have been able to conceive or formulate such speculations in an open and unciphered conceptual language," says Fraenkel in a remarkable book.[22] And in return, philosophy itself, even after the pre-Socratics, continues to draw inspiration from the language of the first cosmogonies.

In sum, then, poetry is always present in prose, because poetry, after all, is not the privilege of poets. A poet is whoever is inspired, whoever speaks as if under the influence of an irresistible constraint and as if he himself were astounded by what he is saying. Suppose that Fabrice should come along and say, "I love you." Then he is being a poet, if these words, so simple and so hackneyed, are somehow torn from him, if they have a strange taste in his mouth, as though pronounced for the first time by the first man, and if they have the power of disclosing to him a new world, in which all things will for a moment be the witnesses and the accomplices of that love. For all speech that is authentic, language is original.

To be sure, not all speech is authentic, but perhaps Heidegger is mistaken in believing that mere talk and chatter are radically unauthentic. Perhaps conversation that is unreflecting and mechanized manages to say something even without realizing it. To talk about the weather is still to evoke the world order; to exchange politenesses is still to adjust oneself to the civic order. The true meaning, of the sort which Heidegger searches for in pre-Socratic oracles, is not abolished in automatisms. Rather it is taken into the current of life, and just how is one to prevent life from being merely an everyday affair? Here I should be inclined to oppose Croce to Heidegger: "Poetry is language in its purest essence. . . . People have thought that this first and poetic language later came to be perverted and degraded into a practical language, a mere utilitarian instrument, and that only the impact of the genius could cause language from time to time to be rediscovered by some of the elect. But no, language is never perverted. . . . Even in the course of lively conversation and in expressions of daily life one can see the words being renewed and invented by the imagination, and then it is that poetry flowers."[23]

Of course, language does tend to become degraded. The linguists show how it tends to wear out on three different levels: on the phonological level, as witnessed by the principle of economy; on the syntactical level, as seen in the simplification of grammatical structures; on the semantic level, as exemplified by what Henle calls the standardization of metaphors. Nevertheless, this falling off is not irremediable: if language grows old, it does not die; there must, indeed, be some way of rejuvenating it. First of all, it can find in the development of the sciences a new rigor and a new richness. A treatise on physics does not chatter along; it speaks in order to say something. It introduces a new language in order to speak a new world, a world humanized by objective concepts and technical procedures—the world of prose, as Hegel called it. Here man has taken the initiative. But this imperialistic attitude of both thought and hands remains based on a more fundamental relation in which man and world are somehow in a state of equality, where the world is not grasped as a system of objects, but lived as a *Lebenswelt*. It is this relation that the natural language establishes.

And precisely, alongside of science, which creates an artificial language, poetry today reanimates the common language by reactivating the primitive language, poetry in its original state. Its means are proper to it. It overturns the everyday language; it disrupts the usual scheme of conveying information. Not only does metaphor bring about unforeseeable alliances between words, but the poetic phrase refuses to be a linear sequence of discrete elements, in order to present itself as a totality in the manner of a melodic phrase.

And yet the procedures of poetry can be paradoxically confronted with those of logic. If the equivocal and insignificant character of the common language can be corrected by the rigor of logical procedure, the same thing can happen through the perfection of poetic form. For there is a poetic formalism just as there is a logical formalism: both assure language of rigor and fullness; both involve rules. In both cases, these rules, which first appear to be arbitrary, prove not to be so, and this confers upon language its truth and veracity. Logical rules are justified by logical laws that constitute a formal ontology and grasp the formal aspect of the world. Rules of prosody are justified by their power to create a new language in which the world can express its many concrete aspects.

It remains that poetry, as an instrument of an original communication between man and world, is the first form of language, the language in which a significance that is still preconceptual is totally immanent in the flesh and blood of words and immediately experienced by feeling. It is the presence itself of the world that is conjured up by speech. All the archaic civilizations have sacralized the power of the Word and honored the voice that proffers it. However, we have not compared logic and poetry merely by chance. The language that binds man to the world is also the language that separates him, which, indeed, is possible only because he is already separated. Reflection that confirms this separation is already potentially in speech. And this appears in modern poetry: it is ever a return to the sources of language; and yet the poet is one who has lost all naïveté. He no longer devotes himself only to evoking and celebrating the world, even when he has recourse to the vocative rather than to the indicative. With Hölderlin, Mallarmé, and T. S. Eliot, he questions himself about his own power and about the meaning of his speech: poetry becomes the poetry of poetry. And so it reveals in its own way that a theory of language must hold the two ends of the chain. Language is the nourishing tie that joins man to the world, and it is also the means for man to emancipate himself and to affirm his will to power. Man can know and become master of things only because he has first named them; and he is able to name them only because they reveal themselves to him, because *Natura naturans* invents language and summons man to speak for himself. That is something which the poet knows and his poetry says: poetry poses the problem of language and offers in its own way a solution to the problem.

Nevertheless, if poetry is the first word, it does not have the last word, for philosophy is still able to meditate on poetry. But poetry does what philosophy can only think: it is not the philosophy of language; it is language itself, original and ever mysterious.

Notes

Foreword

1. Jean Paul Sartre, *L'Être et le néant* (Paris, 1943), p. 116. Translated by Hazel Barnes, *Being and Nothingness* (New York: Philosophical Library, 1956), p. 74.
2. Gilbert Ryle, *The Concept of Mind* (London, 1949), p. 195.
3. Mikel Dufrenne and Paul Ricoeur, *Karl Jaspers et la philosophie de l'existence* (Paris: Éditions de Seuil, 1947).
4. Mikel Dufrenne, *Phénoménologie de l'expérience esthétique* (2 vols.; Paris: Presses Universitaires de France, 1953).
5. Mikel Dufrenne, *La notion d' "a priori"* (Paris: Presses Universitaires de France, 1959).
6. Mikel Dufrenne, *La personalité de base* (Paris, 1953).

Introduction

1. Paul Henle, ed., *Language, Thought and Culture* (Ann Arbor: University of Michigan Press, 1958), p. v.

Chapter 1. Language and Linguistics

1. C. F. Voegelin and Thomas Sebeok, *Results of the Conference of Anthropologists and Linguists* (Bloomington: Indiana University Publications in Anthropology and Linguistics, 1953).
2. Ferdinand de Saussure, *Cours de linguistique générale* (Lausanne: published by Charles Bally and Albert Sechehaye with the collaboration of Albert Riedlinger, 1916), p. 166.

3. The words of Langevin might be recalled in this connection: "The concrete is the abstract rendered familiar through usage. In effect, we define the concrete by the intellectual or practical familiarity that we have with it; everything ends by being concrete; yes, for a hardened mathematician, even the most abstract mathematics is concrete. But inversely, there is no such thing as a pure concrete; the immediate, as Hegel shows in the *Phenomenology of the Mind,* is always mediated; we never go to meet the real empty-handed and without an equipment of essences and aprioris."

4. V. Troubetskoi, *Principes de phonologie,* trans. J. Cantineau (Paris: C. Klincksieck, 1957), p. 40.

5. Leonard Bloomfield, *Language* (New York: Henry Holt and Company, 1933), p. 128.

6. Troubetskoi, *Principes de phonologie,* p. 69.

7. See in this connection the judicious remarks of Robert K. Merton, *Social Theory and Social Structure* (Glencoe, Illinois: Free Press, 1951).

8. André Martinet, *L'Économie des changements phonétiques* (Berne: A. Francke, 1955), p. 42.

9. Troubetskoi, *Principes de phonologie,* p. 41.

10. The application of information theory to the study of language is very clearly presented in George A. Miller's book, *Language and Communication* (New York: McGraw-Hill, 1951).

11. Martinet, *L'Économie* . . . , p. 45.

12. Troubetskoi, *Principes de phonologie,* p. 379.

13. Claude Lévi-Strauss, *Anthropologie structurale* (Paris: Librairie Plon, 1958), p. 230.

14. The use of information theory for the study of learning has been treated most remarkably by J. M. Faverge and A. Ombredane, *L'Analyse de travail* (Paris: Presses Universitaires de France, 1955).

15. Lévi-Strauss, *Anthropologie structurale,* p. 84.

16. F. G. Granger, Évènement et structure dans les sciences de l'homme, *Cahiers de l'Institut de science économique appliquée* (no. 55, 1957), p. 38.

17. Lévi-Strauss, *Anthropologie structurale,* pp. 72–74.

18. In Lévi-Strauss, *Anthropologie structurale.*

Chapter 2. Language and Logic

1. See G. J. Warnock, "Verification and the Use of Language," *Revue internationale de philosophie* (no. 17–18, 1955).

2. See Ernest Gellner, *Words and Things* (London: Gollancz, 1959).

3. Speaking of Strawson as a representative of Oxford philosophy, Morris Weitz writes, "his task is the description of the logic of these uses." "Oxford Philosophy," *Philosophical Review,* LXII (no. 2, April 1953).

4. René Descartes, *Oeuvres choisies*, vol. I (Paris: Garnier, 1930), p. 96.

5. Irving M. Copi gives some excellent examples of this, distinguishing from among the so-called informal fallacies, which are anterior to the intervention of logic, the fallacies of relevance on the one hand, and the fallacies of ambiguity on the other. *Introduction to Logic* (New York: Macmillan, 1953), Chapter III.

6. R. Carnap, *Einführung in die symbolische Logik* (Vienna: Springer, 1954), p. 1.

7. This is the famous principle of tolerance enunciated by R. Carnap: "In logic there are no morals. Everyone is at liberty to build up his own logic, his own forms of language, as he wishes." *The Logical Syntax of Language* (London: Routledge and Kegan Paul, Ltd., 1947), p. 62.

8. Paul Henle, ed., *Language, Thought and Culture* (Ann Arbor: University of Michigan Press, 1958), p. 110.

9. See E. Gilson, *L'Être et l'essence* (Paris: J. Vrin, 1948), *passim*.

10. R. Blanché, *Introduction à la logique contemporaine* (Paris: Colin, 1957), p. 17. A similar analysis of the different uses of the copula may be found as far back as 1924 in Santayana's "Some Meanings of the Word 'Is,' " *Obiter Scripta* (New York: C. Scribner's Sons, 1936).

11. A. N. Whitehead, *An Introduction to Mathematics* (New York: Henry Holt, 1911), p. 61.

12. C. I. Lewis, *An Analysis of Knowledge and Valuation* (La Salle, Illinois: Open Court Publishing Co., 1946), pp. 96–97. H. Veatch, who quotes this passage, makes the following comment upon it: "Thus in constructing a formal system, one is quite at liberty to lay it down as a principle that if x R y, then y R x; or to lay it down that if x R y, then not y R x. However, once a decision has been made respecting one of these alternatives, then one's freedom of choice is over. As a result of that decision one's symbols have taken on a certain meaning, and that meaning is what it is, and its complication and implications are what they are, quite independently of any human decision and regardless of whether any human being ever chooses to entertain that meaning or not." *Intentional Logic* (New Haven: Yale University Press, 1952), p. 51.

13. Suzanne Bachelard, *La logique de Husserl* (Paris: Presses Universitaires de France, 1957), p. 54.

14. Jules Vuillemin, "Le problème phénoménologique: Intentionalité et réflexion," *Revue philosophique* (no. 4, 1959), p. 465.

15. D. Dubarle, *Initiation à la logique mathématique* (Collection de logique mathématique) (Paris: Gauthier-Villars, 1957), p. 36.

16. Jean Ladrière, *Les limitations internes des formalismes* (Louvain: E. Nauwelaerts, 1957), p. 432.

17. *Ibid.*, p. 436.

18. See Edmund Husserl, *Erfahrung und Urteil* (Prague: Academia Verlag, 1939), p. 28.

19. Edmund Husserl, *Formale und transzendentale Logik* (Halle: Max Niemeyer, 1929), p. 167.

20. See *Logische Untersuchungen* vol. II, "the characterization of categorical acts as founded acts" (Halle: 1913).

21. Cited by Veatch, *Intentional Logic*, p. 56.

22. F. G. Granger, "Logique, Langage, Communication," in *Homage à Gaston Bachelard* (Paris: Presses Universitaires de France, 1957), pp. 41 ff.

23. Veatch, *Intentional Logic*, p. 57.

24. Edmund Husserl, *Idées,* trans. Paul Ricoeur (Paris: Gallimard, 1950), p. 40.

25. Quoted in S. Bachelard, *La logique de Husserl,* p. 150.

26. Veatch, *Intentional Logic*, p. 28.

27. Husserl, *Formale und . . .* , p. 186.

Chapter 3. Language and Metaphysics

1. H. Delacroix, E. Cassirer, L. Jordan, et al., *Psychologie du Langage* (Paris: F. Alcan, 1933), pp. 430–496.

2. A. Ombredane, *L'aphasie et l'élaboration de la pensée explicite* (Paris: Presses Universitaires de France, 1951), pp. 369–370.

3. Paul Henle, ed., *Language, Thought and Culture* (Ann Arbor: University of Michigan Press, 1958), p. 133.

4. C. K. Ogden and I. A. Richards, *The Meaning of Meaning,* Supplement I (New York: Harcourt, Brace, 1923), p. 297.

5. Martin Heidegger, *Introduction à la Métaphysique,* trans. G. Kahn (Paris: Presses Universitaires de France, 1958), p. 110.

6. Ogden and Richards, *The Meaning of Meaning,* p. 315.

7. Henle, *Language, Thought and Culture,* p. 168.

8. Maurice Pradines, *Traité de psychologie générale,* t. II (Paris: Presses Universitaires de France, 1946).

9. *Ibid.,* p. 429.

10. See the commentary that Martin Heidegger gives on this passage in *Kant und das Problem der Metaphysik* (Frankfurt: Gerhard Schulte-Bulmke, 1934), pp. 26–27. Translated by James S. Churchill, *Kant and the Problem of Metaphysics* (Bloomington: Indiana University Press, 1962). Even before this, see G. W. F. Hegel, "Glauben und Wissen," in vol. I, *Sämtliche Werke,* ed. Georg Lasson (Leipzig, 1928), p. 241.

11. This sentence from the *Divagations of Mallarmé* finds an echo in a recent phrase of G. Bachelard: "The bouquets of flowers are bouquets of the names of flowers." *La poétique de la rêverie* (Paris: Presses Universitaires de France, 1959), p. 37.

12. Martin Heidegger, *Holzwege* (Frankfurt a. M.: V. Klostermann, 1950), p. 37.

13. Martin Heidegger, *An Introduction to Metaphysics,* trans. Ralph Manheim (New Haven: Yale University Press, 1959), p. 153.

14. *Ibid.,* p. 154.

15. *Ibid.,* p. 153.

16. G. Simondon, *Du mode d'existence des objets techniques* (Paris: Éditions Montaigne, 1958), p. 165.

17. Mircea Eliade, *Traité d'histoire des religions* (Paris: Payot, 1953), p. 47.

18. Clémence Ramnoux, *La nuit et les enfants de la nuit* (Paris: Flammarion, 1959), p. 102.

19. *Ibid.,* p. 44.

20. Carl Jung and K. Kérényi, *Introduction à l'essence de la mythologie,* trans. H. E. Sel Medico (Paris: Payot, 1953), pp. 96, 117.

21. I have attempted to broach this problem of a pre-existent harmony between man and the world in a work devoted to the topic, *La notion d' "a priori"* (Paris: Presses Universitaires de France, 1959).

22. Hermann Fraenkel, *Dichtung und Philosophie des früheren Griechentums* (New York: American Philological Association, 1951), p. 148.

23. Benedetto Croce, *La Poésie,* French trans. D. Dreyfus (Paris: Presses Universitaires de France, 1951), p. 17.